WONDERLAND

NOTES

including
- *Life and Background*
- *List of Characters*
- *Introduction and Brief Synopsis*
- *Summaries and Commentaries*
- *Critical Analysis*
  Alice as a Character
  Abandonment/Loneliness
  The Child-Swain
  Children and Animals
  Death
  Nonsense
  Nature and Nurture
  Justice
  Time and Space
- *Essay Topics*
- *Selected Bibliography*

by
Carl Senna, M.F.A.
Visiting Scholar,
Brown University

Editor

Gary Carey, M.A.
University of Colorado

Consulting Editor

James L. Roberts, Ph.D.
Department of English
University of Nebraska

ISBN 0-8220-0140-3
© Copyright 1984
by
C. K. Hillegass
All Rights Reserved
Printed in U.S.A.

1989 Printing

Cliffs Notes, Inc.   Lincoln, Nebraska

CONTENTS

LIFE AND BACKGROUND 5

    Education 9
    Carroll's Interest in Little Girls 10
    Alice Liddell 11

LIST OF CHARACTERS 12

INTRODUCTION AND BRIEF SYNOPSIS 17

SUMMARIES AND COMMENTARIES

    Down the Rabbit-Hole 26
    The Pool of Tears 29
    A Caucus-Race and a Long Tale 34
    The Rabbit Sends in a Little Bill 36
    Advice from a Caterpillar 38
    Pig and Pepper 42
    A Mad Tea-Party 47
    The Queen's Croquet-Ground 51
    The Mock Turtle's Story, The "Lobster-Quadrille,"
       Who Stole the Tarts?, & Alice's Evidence 52

ALICE AS A CHARACTER 55

THEMES

    Abandonment/Loneliness 57
    The Child-Swain 57
    Children and Animals 58
    Death 58
    Nonsense 59

Nature and Nurture 59
Justice... 60
Time and Space................................. 61

ESSAY QUESTIONS 62

SELECTED BIBLIOGRAPHY 62

ALICE IN WONDERLAND NOTES

LIFE AND BACKGROUND

Of all Lewis Carroll's major works, *Alice in Wonderland* has a unique standing in the category of whimsical, nonsense literature. Much has been written about how this novel contrasts with the vast amount of strict, extremely moralistic children's literature. This is true; *Alice* is quite different from all other Victorian children's literature. Yet, as odd as this story appears in relation to the other Victorian children's stories, this short novel is odder still because it was written by an extremely upright, ultra-conservative man—in short, a quintessential Victorian gentleman.

Lewis Carroll was born Charles Lutwidge Dodgson on January 27, 1832, in the parsonage of Daresbury, Cheshire, England, the third child and eldest son of eleven children of Reverend Charles Dodgson and his wife, Francis Jane Lutwidge. The parents were descended from two ancient and distinguished North Country families. From the Dodgsons, the son inherited a very old tradition of service to the Church and a tradition that he belonged to one of the most respected lineages in England—for example, family legend has it that King James I actually "knighted" either a loin of beef or mutton at the table of Sir Richard Houghton, one of Carroll's ancestors. This incident has been thought by some critics to have inspired the introductory lines in *Through the Looking Glass,* the sequel to *Alice in Wonderland,* when the Red Queen introduces the leg of mutton to Alice: "Alice—Mutton: Mutton—Alice."

For the sake of those who are curious about pen names and how authors choose one over another, "Lewis Carroll" is an interesting example. While teaching at Christ Church, Oxford, Charles Dodgson (Carroll) wrote comic literature and parodies for a humorous paper, *The Train.* The first of the several pieces submitted to *The Train* was signed "B. B." It was so popular that the editor asked Dodgson to use a proper nom de plume; at first, Dodgson proposed "Dares," after his birthplace, Daresbury. The editor thought that the name was too journalistic, so after struggling over a number of choices, Dodgson wrote to his editor and suggested a number of variations and anagrams, based on the letters of his actual name. "Lewis Carroll" was finally decided on, derived from a rearrangement of most of the letters in the name "Charles Lutwidge Dodgson." Clearly, Carroll was fascinated with anagrams, and he will use them throughout *Alice in Wonderland*; his interest in anagrams also explains much about the writings in his later life, and his mathematical works. Concerning Carroll, one cannot safely exclude any influence, least of all hereditary ones, but a good case can be made for the formative effect of Carroll's father on him. Those who knew Reverend Dodgson said that he was a pious and gloomy man, almost devoid of any sense of humor. Yet from his letters to his son, there is recorded evidence of a *remarkable* sense of fun. For example, in one letter to his son, he speaks of screaming in the middle of a street:

> "Iron-mongers-Iron-mongers—Six hundred men
> will rush out of their shops in a moment—fly, fly,
> in all directions—ring the bells, call the constables—
> set the town on fire. I will have a file & a screwdriver,
> & a ring, & if they are not brought directly, in forty
> seconds I will leave nothing but one small cat alive
> in the whole town of Leeds, & I shall only leave that
> because I shall not have time to kill it.

To a boy of eight, such correspondence from his father must have greatly heightened his later love for literary exaggeration; indeed, such fanciful letters may have been the genesis for Carroll's so-called nonsense books.

As we noted, Reverend Dodgson was said to be an austere, puritanical, and authoritarian Victorian man; Lewis Carroll's mother, however, was the essence of the Victorian "gentlewoman." As described by her son, she was "one of the sweetest and gentlest women that had ever lived, whom to know was to love." The childhood of Lewis Carroll was relatively pleasant, full of ideas and hobbies that contributed to his future creative works. His life at Daresbury was secluded, though, and his playmates were mostly his brothers and sisters. Class distinctions did not permit much socializing between children of the parsonage and the "lesser" parish children. Curiously, a number of the Dodgson children, including Carroll, stammered severely. More than one author has suggested that, at least in Carroll's case, his stammer may have arisen from his parents' attempts to correct his left-handedness. Isa Bowman, a childhood friend of Carroll's, has said that whenever adults approached them on their walks, Carroll's speech became extremely difficult to understand. Apparently, he panicked; his shyness and stammering always seemed worse when he was in the world of adults. This stammering made him into a bit of a "loner" and explains, somewhat, Carroll's longtime fascination with puzzles and anagrams, solitary games to amuse himself. It was as though the long suppressed, left-handed self endured in the fanciful, literary adult Carroll—in contrast to the very stern adult librarian, mathematics lecturer, deacon, dormitory master, and curator of the dining hall. Carroll was, seemingly, the archetype of the left-handed man in a right-handed world, like his own White Knight in *Through the Looking Glass* (the sequel to *Alice in Wonderland*).

"And now if ever by chance I put
My fingers into glue
Or madly squeeze a right-hand foot
Into a left-hand shoe . . ."

Carroll's fondness for games, language puzzles, and the world of the bizarre is further demonstrated in his flair for amusing his brothers and sisters—especially his sisters, which explains, perhaps, his lifelong attraction for little girls. In fact, a great deal of Carroll's childhood was spent taking care of his little sisters. At home, it was he who was in charge of these seven sisters, and his imagination was constantly being exercised in order to entertain them. In one of his fanciful story-games that he invented, he imagined a sort of "railway game," and as one of the rules of the game, at least *three* trains had to run over the passengers in order for the passengers to be attended to by physicians. Fortunately, though, rarely were Carroll's amusements cruel, and when the family moved to the Croft Rectory, Yorkshire, where Carroll's father assumed the Archdeaconry, Carroll wrote, directed, and performed light, gay plays, and he also manipulated puppets and marionettes for his family and friends.

In addition to the plays that Carroll wrote and the scripts that he composed for his puppet theater, he also wrote poems, stories, and humorous sketches for his own "magazines." In his "Useful and Instructive Poetry" magazine, for example, a volume that was composed for a younger brother and a sister, he satirized a copybook of stern, dogmatic maxims (a typical Victorian children's book), and in this poem, he alluded to his own handicap:

> "Learn well your grammar
> And never stammer . . . .
> Eat bread with butter;
> Once more, don't stutter."

Other poems in the volume focus on the theme of fairy tales, an interest which played a large part in the creation of *Alice*. An early poem of Carroll's, for instance, "My Fairy," suggests the contrariness of the creatures that Alice will meet in Wonderland:

> "I have a fairy by my side
> Which cried; it said, 'You must not weep.'
> If, full of mirth, I smile and grin,
> It says, 'You must not laugh,'
> When once I wished to drink some gin,
> It said, 'You must not quaff.' "

Similarly, in another early poem, "A Tale of a Tail," there is a drawing of a very long dog's tail, suggestive of the very slender, increasingly smaller mouse's tail in *Alice*, which coils across a single page in a sort of S-shape. Also, an early poem about someone falling off a wall anticipates Humpty Dumpty in *Through the Looking Glass*, and a "Morals" essay reminds one of the ridiculous conversations between the ugly Duchess and the evil Queen in *Alice*. It is difficult to ignore the writings of Carroll as a child in any analysis of his works, for in his childhood productions, we find conclusive evidence of early imitations, hints, allusions, suggestions, and actual elements of imaginary creatures, dreams, and visions that will appear in his later works.

EDUCATION

All his life, Carroll was a scholar; when he was not a student, he was a teacher, and until two years before his death, he was firmly imbedded in the life of Oxford University. Quite honestly, though, nothing very exciting ever happened in Carroll's life, apart from a trip to the Continent, including Russia. His vacations were all local ones, to his sister's home in Guildford, his aunt's home in Hastings, and to Eastbourne, the Lake Country, and Wales. He did not begin his formal schooling until the age of twelve, when he enrolled in Richmond Grammar School, ten miles from the Croft Rectory, but he had already received a thorough background in literature from the family library. Yet it was mathematics – and not English literature – that interested Carroll most. When he was very young, for example, Carroll implored his father to explain logarithms to him, presumably because he had already mastered arithmetic, algebra, and even most of Euclidian geometry.

Carroll entered Rugby in 1846, but the sensitive young child found the all-boys environment highly unpleasant; the bullying abuse, the flogging, and the caning was a daily part of school life. Nonetheless, Carroll was, despite his three years of unhappiness there, an exceedingly studious boy, and he won many prizes for academic excellence.

Carroll matriculated at Christ Church, Oxford, in 1851, and remained there for forty-seven years. But, two days after entering Oxford, he received word of his mother's death, something which deeply distressed him and seemed to have worsened his stammering. By all accounts, Carroll was not an outgoing student; with little money, and because of his stammer, his circle of friends always remained small. Yet in his academic work, he applied himself with the same energy and devotion that characterized his career at Rugby. He won scholarship prizes, honors in Classical exams, and also won a First Prize in Mathematics. His scholastic efforts were rewarded by a lifetime fellowship and a residency at Christ Church, so long as he remained unmarried and proceeded to take Holy Orders.

In 1854, the year Carroll took his B.A. degree, he began publishing poetry in the student magazines and in *The Whitby Gazette*. Carroll's writings had already established him as both a superb raconteur and humorist at Oxford, and in 1854, he began to seriously teach himself how to express his thoughts in proper literary form; it was at that time that his writings began to show some of the whimsy and fantasy that are contained in the *Alice* books.

In 1857, Carroll took his M.A. degree and was made "Master of the House." During those years, he immersed himself in literature, mathematics, and also in the London theater. He produced free-lance humorous prose pieces and verses for various periodicals, explored theories of dual identities, wrote satires, published mathematical and symbolic logic texts, invented word games and puzzles, and took up photography, a hobby that would make him famous as one of the best Victorian photographers. In short, Carroll became a sort of lesser English equivalent of Leonardo da Vinci. He invented the Nyctograph, a device for writing in the dark, and he also invented a method of remote control self-photography. Helmut Gernshein, the author of *Lewis Carroll: Photographer,* calls Carroll's photographic achievements "astonishing"; in his estimation, Carroll "must not only rank as a pioneer of British amateur photography, but I would also unhesitatingly acclaim him as the most outstanding photographer of children in the nineteenth century."

CARROLL'S INTEREST IN LITTLE GIRLS

In every study of Carroll's life, one finds that Carroll had only the most formal encounters with mature women. There was seemingly no romantic interest in adult women. Some biographers have attributed this asexual interest to Carroll's stammering and his self-conscious shyness about it. On the other hand, Carroll's diaries and contemporary accounts about him are full of his encounters with children, nearly always with little girls. He obviously delighted in the company of little girls twelve years old and younger, and his diary records in great detail the aesthetic pleasure that he took in viewing "nice little children." Carroll's attractions for little girls were honorable and above reproach – at least we have, almost a century later, absolutely no evidence to the contrary.

Carroll's interest in discovering new little girls for his photographic studio seems to have amounted to his discovering hundreds, perhaps thousands, of girls in his lifetime. And in nearly every recorded case, Carroll produced a masterpiece of character study. His photographs are filled with unusually sensitive and candid "personalities" of the subjects. They caught the essence of human beings; they were not merely stiff, embalmed-like "objects." Occasionally, there is an extraordinary sense of straightforward eroticism – but it is straightforward; it is not murky or perverted. And in nearly every recorded case, Carroll had the full approbation of the child's parents, and invariably his work was chaperoned, at least indirectly. Had there been any intimacies between Carroll and his young female subjects, it would long ago have been ferreted out by the multitude of Freudian-oriented literary critics.

Today, we can understand why, occasionally, certain people thought Carroll's photographs to be erotic. Most people now, however, wouldn't consider them to be. His photographs are alluring; they look as if they almost could speak. They all have a provocative quality about them. But, they are "safe," and as we view them, they help us to understand Carroll's interest in seeing children as *his own* personal, private, peculiar *escape* from mature sex.

ALICE LIDDELL

In 1856, Carroll met Alice Liddell, the four-year-old daughter of Dean Henry George Liddell of Christ Church. Carroll had already established himself as a close friend of Alice's elder sister and cousin. But it is Alice who figures most prominently in Carroll's most famous creation, *Alice in Wonderland.*

On July 4, 1852, Carroll and a friend, Rev. Robinson Duckworth, took the Liddell children, Lorina (13), Alice (10), and Edith (8) on a boat ride (a row boat) up the Isis River (the local name for the Thames River). As they made their way upstream, Carroll began telling a story about the underground adventures of a little girl named Alice. According to Duckworth, the story "was actually composed and spoken over my shoulder for the benefit of Alice Liddell, who was acting as 'cox' of our gig. I remember turning around and saying, 'Dodgson, is this an extempore romance of yours?' And he replied, 'Yes, I'm inventing as we go along.'"

Upon disembarking, Alice asked Carroll to write out Alice's adventures for her, and Carroll promised to do so by the following Christmas, but the work was not completed until February 10, 1863. By that time, Alice was eleven, and Carroll was no longer seeing her with the regularity that he used to. Now he had made a new friend, the famous ingénue Ellen Terry, who was nearly seventeen. His interest in Ellen Terry is the closest relationship that Carroll had with an adult woman, apart from his family, of course.

From an initial length of 18,000 words, Carroll's manuscript expanded to 35,000 words, and the famous English illustrator John Tenniel read it and consented to draw illustrations for it. As Carroll searched for a publisher, he gave anxious thoughts to a perfect title. Various ones came to him: *Alice's Golden Hour, Alice's Hour in Elf-land, Alice Among the Elves, Alice's Doings in Elf-land,* and *Alice's Adventures Under Ground.* Finally, *Alice in Wonderland* was chosen, and Macmillan, the publishers for Oxford University, agreed to publish the book on a commission basis.

Alice was an immediate critical success when it appeared in 1865. *The Reader* magazine called it "a glorious artistic treasure . . . a book to put on one's shelf as an antidote to a fit of the blues." *The Pall Mall Gazette* wrote that "this delightful little book is a children's feast and a triumph of nonsense." About 180,000 copies of *Alice* in various editions were sold in England during Carroll's lifetime; by 1911, there were almost 700,000 copies in print. Since then, with the expiration of the original copyright in 1907, the book has been translated into every major language, and now it has become a perennial best-seller, ranking with the works of Shakespeare and the Bible in popular demand. In the words of the critic Derek Hudson: "The most remarkable thing about *Alice* is that, though it springs from the very heart of the Victorian period, it is timeless in its appeal. This is a characteristic that it shares with other classics – a small band – that have similarly conquered the world."

LIST OF CHARACTERS

Alice

The heroine and the dreamer of Wonderland; she is the principal character.

Alice's Sister

She reads the book "without pictures or conversations." Alice's boredom with her sister's book leads her to fall asleep and dream her adventures in Wonderland.

White Rabbit

The first creature that Alice sees in Wonderland. He leads Alice down the hole to Wonderland; he mistakes Alice for his servant, Mary Ann, and he orders her to fetch his gloves and fan. He is the Court Herald for the Knave of Hearts' trial.

Mouse

The first creature that Alice sees while she is floating in a pool of her own tears. The Mouse offers to dry all of the creatures by telling them about "dry" history. He tells Alice his own sad tale, and it is presented on the page in the shape of a mouse's tail.

Duck

One of the menagerie in the pool of tears. He argues with the Mouse over the meaning of "it."

Dodo

One of the animals in the pool of tears; he proposes the Caucus-race.

Lory (parrot)

Animal in the pool of tears. He argues with Alice over his authority and refuses to reveal his age.

Eaglet

Animal in the pool of tears.

Old Crab

Animal in the pool of tears.

Old Magpie

Another animal in the pool of tears.

Canary

Animal in the pool of tears. The Canary takes offense at Alice's describing her pet cat Dinah's appetite for birds.

Dinah

Alice's pet cat, who lives above-ground.

Pat

The White Rabbit's servant. He is ordered to evict Alice from the White Rabbit's house, but he gets Bill the Lizard to go into the house instead. Pat speaks with a brogue.

Young Bill the Lizard

The other servant of the White Rabbit; he makes an unsuccessful attempt to evict Alice from the White Rabbit's house.

Puppy

One of the nonpersonified or unanimated animals; he is of monstrous size (to Alice), and he almost crushes Alice in his playfulness after she flees from the White Rabbit's house.

Caterpillar

The water-pipe smoking character whom Alice finds on a mushroom. He is disagreeable and insulting to Alice. But he provides her with knowledge of the growth-altering mushroom.

Father William

An old man who is the subject of the misconceived poem that the Caterpillar asks Alice to recite. Instead of an ethical "model" for youths, Father William becomes, in Alice's recital of the moral poem, a corrupt figure.

Father William's Son

The inquiring son of Father William.

Pigeon

The pigeon hen attacks Alice because Alice's neck has been distorted by the mushroom into a serpent's shape. The pigeon's mis-identity of Alice is strengthened when she confesses to eating eggs when she was above-ground. The pigeon confuses a part of Alice (Alice's neck and her taste for eggs) for what he considers to be the "identifying quality" of a serpent.

Fish-Footman

Servant of the Queen of Hearts who delivers the Queen's invitation (for the croquet party) to the Duchess.

Frog-Footman

Doorman of the Duchess' house. He receives the Queen's croquet party invitation for the Duchess. He banters nonsense – with variations – to Alice.

Duchess

Mad human character of hideous physical aspect and perverse disposition. She abuses the pig/baby and throws it to Alice. Later, she moralizes with Alice at the croquet party. She flees the garden after offending the Queen of Hearts. Earlier, the Duchess was arrested and imprisoned, under an execution sentence, for having boxed the Queen's ears.

Cook

Duchess' cook. She throws pots and plates about, but doesn't hit anyone, although one plate grazes the Frog-Footman's nose. Her indiscriminate shaking of a pepper mill causes everyone in the Duchess' house to sneeze, especially the pig/baby, who screams and cries.

Cheshire-Cat

It first appears in the kitchen with the Duchess, the Cook, and the pig/baby. The Cat is always smiling. After leaving the Duchess' house, Alice finds the Cat on a tree limb. Alice tries to engage him in a serious conversation, but he replies to her in nonsense questions and answers. He vanishes and reappears, and sometimes only his head, or his enigmatic smile, is visible. In the next to the last chapter, he frustrates the Queen and the King of Hearts' order to execute him by making only his head visible – thus, there is no head to cut off. He directs Alice to the March Hare's Mad Tea-Party.

March Hare

Host of the Mad Tea-Party. He and another guest, the Mad Hatter, try to drown the third guest-resident, the Dormouse.

The Mad Hatter

Another guest-resident at the Mad Tea-Party. He explains to Alice why the tea-party is always held at six o'clock and why the time is *always* six o'clock. The Hatter and a personified Time have had a fight, and Time refuses to let the tea-party end. The Hatter is interrogated by the King at the Knave of Hearts' trial; he and the March Hare dunk the Dormouse in the teapot.

Dormouse

A hibernating guest-resident at the Mad Tea-Party. He tells anecdotes of three sisters who live in a treacle well and draw treacle. He is dunked in the teapot by the Mad Hatter and the March Hare. He is barely able to stay awake, but appears later at the Knave's trial.

Spade Gardeners

The Two, the Five, and the Seven of Spades; animated playing cards. They are "gardeners" for the Queen of Hearts. Alice finds them painting white roses red. Alice saves them from execution when the Queen orders them beheaded.

King of Hearts

He is the Queen's husband and also the judge at the trial of the Knave of Hearts.

Queen of Hearts

The furious queen of the enchanted garden. She is the real power behind Wonderland. Her violent and outrageous temper provokes Alice to overturn Wonderland and return to the world above-ground. The Queen introduces Alice to the Gryphon.

Knave of Hearts

The only "person" in Wonderland to evoke Alice's sympathy. He is accused of stealing tarts in the enchanted garden. Alice saves him from the queen's wrath and execution.

Three Sisters

Three little girls whom the Dormouse describes as living in the treacle well.

Mock Turtle

A sad "mock turtle" who used to be a tortoise; he regales Alice with accounts of his peculiar education. He recites the "Lobster-Quadrille." The Mock Turtle's name means "veal," a name that reflects the meaning of his lugubrious verse. He and the Gryphon are not overly hostile or rude to Alice.

Gryphon (Griffin)

A mythical creature who takes Alice to the Mock Turtle. He is introduced to Alice by the queen. He is polite to Alice and is never overtly hostile.

Guinea Pigs

Part of the inefficient jury at the Knave of Hearts' trial.

Pig/Baby

An "infant" whom Alice takes pity on when she sees it being cruelly tested by the Duchess. As Alice is escaping with it, it turns into a baby pig.

Mary Ann

Servant of the White Rabbit.

INTRODUCTION AND BRIEF SYNOPSIS

Alice was the work of a mathematician and logician who wrote as both a humorist and as a limerist. The story was in no sense intended to be didactic; its only purpose was to entertain. One may look for Freudian or Jungian interpretations if one chooses to do so, but in the final analysis, the story functions as comedy, with dialogue used largely for Carroll to play on words, mixing fantasy with burlesque actions. The success of *Alice* (1865) enabled Carroll to forego his activities as a deacon. After the death of his deeply religious father in 1868, Carroll was able to propose a one-third cut in his salary as a mathematical lecturer. His most famous mathematical work, *Euclid and His Modern Rivals*, had been published the year before, and in 1881, he proposed to resign his academic post so that he could give full time to writing and pursuing mathematical studies. But in 1882, he was made Curator of the Common Room and was persuaded to remain there until 1892. He continued to write on mathematical topics and completed the first volume of his *Symbolic Logic*. By then, he was independently wealthy as a result of his many successful publications: *Phantasmagoria* appeared in 1869; in 1871, *Through the Looking Glass* came out; in 1876, *The Hunting of the Snark* appeared, and in 1883, *Rhyme and Reason* was published. Carroll's university responsibilities broadened in those years and from time to time he even accepted a request for a sermon. Though his authorship of the *Alice* books was well known, he absolutely shunned *all* publicity and refused to acknowledge any connection to "Lewis Carroll."

After leaving Oxford, Carroll settled into his sister's house in Guildford. And there he died in the afternoon of January 14, 1898. His memory is preserved in a perpetual endowment of a cot in the Children's Hospital, Great Ormond Street, London. In the long run, his books for children, especially the *Alice* books, have taken their place as books worthy of serious study of English literature. Thus, almost ironically, the so-called nonsense writer's achievements are timeless and unchallengeable, and the fame of *Alice* endures.

To fully appreciate *Alice*, one must keep in mind that the whole is simpler than its parts, and that although it was written originally for children, *Alice* has become a favorite adult piece of literature, a critical and philosophical work, rich in multiple meanings. More scholars (particularly economists and mathematicians) seem to allude to the *Alice* books with each passing day. The broad appeal of *Alice*, then, certainly lends substance to the notion that Alice and the novel are, ultimately, what you make of them. But there is some question as to whether children enjoy the puzzlement found in the story's episodes more than the story itself. In any case, children do not need critical information to appreciate *Alice*. The philosophical allusions and psychological implications are for adult tastes.

As a work of fiction, *Alice* lacks the conventional story line that we normally associate with a coherent, unified tale. Yet reading *Alice* does not leave us with a sense of incompleteness; *Alice* is far more than merely a series of disconnected episodes. In fact, *Alice* is told in the form of a dream; it is the story of Alice's dream, told in the third person point-of-view. Because Carroll chose a dream as the structure for his story, he was free to make fun of and satirize the multitudes of standard Victorian didactic maxims in children's literature. *Alice* lacks a "morally good" heroine and meaning; instead of Carroll's making an ethical point about each of her adventures (and showing how "good little girls" should behave in a situation just described), *Alice* parodies the instructive, solemn verse which filled Victorian children's books, verses which children were made to *memorize* and *recite.*

Alice, however, is not intended to *instruct* children in points of religion, morality, etiquette, and growing up to be mature, reasonable adults. In this novel, conventional "rationality" is replaced by the bizarre, fantastic irrationalities of a dream world. From episode to episode, Alice never progresses to any *rational* understanding or mental or psychological growth. Her adventures are *not* ordered; they are disordered. They are shifting and unpredictable, and there is always the menace of Gothic horror laced with the fantasies of Carroll's fairy tale. Indeed, Alice's dream sometimes has the aspects of a nightmare.

Wonderland is a world of wonders, a world where fairy or elf-like creatures and humans meet and talk with one another. Wonderland is a world where a baby is transformed into a pig; it is a place where a Cheshire-Cat keeps disappearing and reappearing, until only his grin remains—and even that suddenly disappears! Wonderland is a kingdom in which the Queen and King of Hearts have subjects who are a deck of cards, and where *all* the animals (except the pig/baby) have the nagging, whining, complaining, and peevish attitudes of adults. It is as though Carroll were trying to frustrate *logical* communication and trying to turn extraordinary events into what would seem like very ordinary events in Wonderland. The only laws in *Alice* seem to be the laws of chaos; all is nonsensical. Yet, one of the novel's key focuses is on the relationship between the development of a child's language and the physical growth of the child. In Wonderland, illogical and irrational Wonderland, sudden size change has a distorting psychological effect on Alice, and this is made even more mysterious by the verbal nonsense that accompanies it. This dream magic mesmerizes children, and it makes them laugh. Most adults do not. To break a law of logic is serious business to adults; children, however, love the wildly improbable.

In any case, most of the humor in *Alice* is due to the fact that the reader has the privileged knowledge that Alice is *dreaming*; thus, she *should not* assume that anything in Wonderland should function as it does in the real world. Wonderland is a sort of reverse utopia, a decadent, corrupted one.

Many years ago, Swiss child psychologist Jean Piaget demonstrated that children learn in stages and that before a certain mental age, a child will not be able to comprehend certain *abstract* relationships. Carroll seems to have already grasped this principle and is playing with the notion in this novel. Alice changes in size, but she *never matures*. The solemn adult creatures whom she meets speak to her, but what they say to her seems like absolute nonsense — that is, Carroll was satirizing the pseudo-intellectuality of adults in the Victorian world he saw all around him. And part of Alice's problem is that none of the nonsense *ever* makes sense; she never learns *anything*, even when she physically grows, or wanders through Wonderland's garden meeting people and creatures.

She grows nine feet tall after eating a cake in the opening chapter, yet she remains a child. Presumably, Alice would have continued to be baffled forever, so long as she remained in Wonderland. She is trapped in the midst of a vacuous condition, without beginning or end, without resolution.

The novel is composed of twelve brief chapters; it can be read in an afternoon. Each of the brief chapters, furthermore, is divided into small, individual, almost isolated episodes. And the story begins with Alice and her sister sitting on the bank of a river reading a book which has no pictures or dialogue in it. ". . . and what is the use of a book," thought Alice, "without pictures or conversations?" Thus, we find many pictures and read much dialogue (although very little of it makes sense) in *this* novel.

After introducing us to one of the creatures in Wonderland, the Gryphon, for instance, the narrator tells us, "If you don't know what a Gryphon is, look at the picture." As noted earlier, Wonderland is filled with strange animals, and Alice's encounters with these creatures, all of whom engage her in conversations, confuse her even more whenever she meets yet another inhabitant of this strange country.

Slowly losing interest in her sister's book, Alice catches sight of a white rabbit. However, he is not merely a rabbit; he will be the "White Rabbit," a major character in the novel. In this first paragraph, then, we learn about the protagonist, Alice, her age, her temperament, and the setting and the mood of the story. In a dream, Alice has escaped from the dull and boring and prosaic world of adulthood—a world of dull prose and pictureless experiences; she has entered what seems to be a confusing, but perpetual springtime of physical, if often terrifying, immediacy.

The White Rabbit wears a waistcoat, walks upright, speaks English, and is worrying over the time on his pocket watch. Alice follows him simply because she is very curious about him. And very soon she finds herself falling down a deep tunnel. For a few minutes, she is frightened; the experience of falling disorients her. Soon, however, she realizes that she is not falling fast; instead, she is falling in a slow, almost floating descent. As she falls, she notices that the tunnel walls are lined with cupboards, bookshelves, maps, and paintings. She takes a jar of orange marmalade off a shelf. But finding the jar empty, she replaces it on a lower shelf, as though she were trying to maintain a sense of some propriety—especially in this situation of absolute uncertainty. As she reflects on the marmalade jar, she says that had she dropped the jar, she might have killed someone below. Alice is clearly a self-reflective young girl—and she's also relatively calm; her thinking reveals a curiously mature mind at times. But like an ordinary little girl, she feels homesick for her cat, Dinah. In that respect, she is in sharp contrast with conventional child heroines of the time. Although Alice may be curious and sometimes bewildered, she is never *too* nice or *too* naughty. But she is always aware of her class-status as a "lady." At one point, she even fears that some of Wonderland's creatures have confused her for a servant, as when the White Rabbit thinks that she is his housekeeper, Mary Ann, and orders Alice to fetch his gloves and fan.

Thus, in Chapter I, Carroll prepares us for Alice's first major confrontation with absolute chaos. And note that Alice's literal-minded reaction to the *impossible* is always considered absurd here in Wonderland; it is laughable, yet it is her only way of coping. As she falls through the rabbit-hole, for instance, she wonders what latitude or longitude she has arrived at. This is humorous and ridiculous because such measurements – if one stops to think about it – are *meaningless* words to a seven-year-old girl, and they are certainly meaningless measurements of *anything* underground.

In Chapter II, Alice finds herself still in the long passageway, and the White Rabbit appears and goes off into a long, low hall full of locked doors. Behind one very small door, Alice remembers that there is "the loveliest garden you ever saw" (remember, she saw this in Chapter I), but now she has drunk a liquid that has made her too large to squeeze even her head through the doorway of the garden. She wishes that she could fold herself up like a telescope and enter. This wish becomes possible when she finds a shrinking potion and a key to the door. The potion reduces her to ten inches high, but she forgets to take the key with her (!) before shrinking, and now the table is too high for her to reach the key. To any young child, this is silly and something to be laughted at, but on another level, there's an element of fear; for children, the predictable proportions of things are important matters of survival. Yet here in Wonderland, things change – for no known reason – thus, logic has lost all its validity.

Then Alice eats a cake that she finds, and her neck shoots up until it resembles a giraffe's. Suddenly, she is a distorted nine feet tall! Clearly, her ability to change size has been a mixed blessing. In despair, she asks, "Who in the world am I?" This is a key question.

Meanwhile, the rapid, haphazard nature of Alice's physical and emotional changes have created a dangerous pool of tears that almost causes her to drown when she shrinks again. Why has she shrunk? She realizes that she has been holding the White Rabbit's lost white gloves and fan – therefore, it *must* be the magic of the fan that is causing her to shrink to almost nothingness. She saves herself by instantly dropping the fan. But now she is desperate; in vain, she searches her mind for something to make sense out of all this illogical chaos, something like arithmetic and geography, subjects that are solid, lasting, and rational. But even they seem to be confused because no matter how much she recites their rules, nothing helps. At the close of this chapter, she is swimming desperately in a pool of her own tears, alongside a mouse and other chattering creatures that have suddenly, somehow, appeared. *Alice in Wonderland* is full of parody and satire. And in Chapter III, Victorian history is Carroll's target. The mouse offers to *dry* the other creatures and Alice by telling them a *very dry* history of England. Then, Carroll attacks politics: the Dodo organizes a Caucus-race, a special race in which every participant wins a prize. Alice then learns the mouse's sad tale as Carroll's editor narrates it on the page in the shape of a mouse's very narrow, S-shaped tail. The assembled, unearthly creatures cannot accept ordinary language, and so Alice experiences, again, absolute bafflement; this is linguistic and semantic disaster. Indeed, much of the humor of this chapter is based on Alice's reactions to the collapse of three above-ground assumptions: predictable growth, an absolute distinction between animals and humans, and an identity that remains constant. We might also add to the concept of a constancy of identity a conformity of word usage. But in Wonderland, Alice's previous identity and the very concept of a permanent identity has repeatedly been destroyed, just as the principles of above-ground are contradicted everywhere; here in Wonderland, such things as space, size, and even arithmetic are shown to have *no consistent laws.*

In Chapter IV, the confusion of identity continues. The White Rabbit insists that Alice fetch him his gloves and his fan. Somehow, he thinks that Alice is his servant, and Alice, instead of objecting to his confusion, passively accepts her new role, just as she would obey an adult ordering her about above-ground. On this day when everything has gone wrong, she feels absolutely defeated.

In the rabbit's house, Alice finds and drinks another growth potion. This time, however, she becomes so enormous that she fills up the room so entirely that she can't get out. These continuing changes in size illustrate her confused, rapid identity crisis and her continuous perplexity. After repulsing the rabbit's manservant, young Bill, a Lizard (who is trying to evict her), Alice notices that pebbles that are being thrown at her through a window are turning into *cakes.* Upon eating one of them, she shrinks until she is small enough to escape the rabbit's house and hide in a thick wood.

In Chapter V, "Advice From a Caterpillar," Alice meets a rude Caterpillar; pompously and dogmatically, he states that she must keep her temper – which is even more confusing to her for she is a little irritable because she simply cannot make any *sense* in this world of Wonderland. Alice then becomes more polite, but the Caterpillar only sharpens his already very short, brusque replies. In Wonderland, there are obviously no conventional rules of etiquette. Thus, Alice's attempt at politeness and the observance of social niceties are still frustrated attempts of hers to react as well as she can to very unconventional behavior – at least, it's certainly unconventional according to the rules that she learned above-ground.

Later, Alice suffers another bout of "giraffe's neck" from nibbling one side of the mushroom that the Caterpillar was sitting on. The effect of this spurt upward causes her to be mistaken for an egg-eating serpent by an angry, vicious pigeon.

In Chapters VI and VII, Alice meets the foul-tempered Duchess, a baby that slowly changes into a pig, the famous, grinning Cheshire-Cat, the March Hare, the Mad Hatter, and the very, very sleepy Dormouse. The latter three are literally trapped (although they don't know it) in a time-warp – trapped in a *perpetual* time when tea is being forever served. Life is one long tea-party, and this episode is Carroll's assault on the notion of time. At the tea-party, it is *always* teatime; the Mad Hatter's watch tells the *day* of the year, but not the *time* since it is *always* six o'clock. At this point, it is important that you notice a key aspect of Wonderland; here, *all* these creatures treat Alice (and her reactions) as though *she* is insane – and as though *they* are sane! In addition, when they are not condescending to her or severely criticizing her, the creatures continually contradict her. And Alice passively presumes the fault to be hers – in almost every case – because all of the creatures act as though their madness is normal and not at all unusual. It is the logical Alice who is the queer one. The chapter ends with Alice at last entering the garden by eating more of the mushroom that the Caterpillar was sitting on. Alice is now about a foot tall.

Chapters VIII to X introduce Alice to the most grimly evil and most irrational people (and actions) in the novel. Alice meets the sovereigns of Wonderland, who display a perversely hilarious rudeness not matched by anyone except possibly by the old screaming Duchess. The garden is inhabited by playing cards (with arms and legs and heads),who are ruled over by the barbarous Queen of Hearts. The Queen's constant refrain and response to seemingly *all* situations is: "Off with their heads!" This beautiful garden, Alice discovers, is the

Queen's private croquet ground, and the Queen matter-of-factly orders Alice to play croquet. Alice's confusion now turns to fear. Then she meets the ugly Duchess again, as well as the White Rabbit, the Cheshire-Cat, and a Gryphon introduces her to a Mock Turtle, who sings her a sad tale of his mock (empty) education; then the Mock Turtle teaches her and the Gryphon a dance called the "Lobster-Quadrille." Chapters XI and XII concern the trial of the Knave of Hearts. Here, Alice plays a heroic role at the trial, and she emerges from Wonderland and awakens to reality. The last two chapters represent the overthrow of Wonderland and Alice's triumphant rebellion against the mayhem and madness that she experienced while she was lost, for awhile, in the strange world of Wonderland.

This story is characterized, first of all, by Alice's unthinking, irrational, and heedless jumping down the rabbit-hole, an act which is at once superhuman and beyond human experience — but Alice does it. And once we accept this premise, we are ready for the rest of the absurdities of Wonderland and Alice's attempts to understand it and, finally, to escape from it. Confusion begins almost immediately because Alice tries to use her world of knowledge from the adult world above-ground in order to understand this new world. Wonderland, however, is a lawless world of deepest, bizarre dream unconsciousness, and Alice's journey through it is a metaphorical search for experience. What she discovers in her dream, though, is a more meaningful and terrifying world than most conscious acts of intelligence would ever lead her to. Hence, "Who in the world am I?" is Alice's constant, confused refrain, one which people "above-ground" ask themselves many, many times throughout their lifetimes.

Throughout the story, Alice is confronted with the problem of shifting identity, as well as being confronted with the anarchy and by the cruelty of Wonderland. When Alice physically shrinks in size, she is never really small enough to hide from the disagreeable creatures that she meets; yet when she grows to adult or to even larger size, she is still not large enough to command authority. "There are things in *Alice*," writes critic William Empson, "that would give Freud the creeps." Often we find poor Alice (and she is often described as being either "poor" or "curious") in tears over something that the adult reader finds comic. And "poor Alice" is on the verge of tears most of the time. When she rarely prepares to laugh, she is usually checked by the morbid, humorless types of creatures whom she encounters in Wonderland. Not even the smiling Cheshire-Cat is kind to her. Such a hostile breakdown of the ordinary world is *never* funny to the child, however comic it might appear to adults. But then Wonderland would not be so amusing to us except in terms of its sheer, unabated madness.

One of the central concerns of *Alice* is the subject of growing up — the anxieties and the mysteries of personal identity as one matures. When Alice finds her neck elongated, everything, in her words, becomes "queer"; again, *she is uncertain who she is.* As is the case with most children, Alice's identity depends upon her control of her body. Until now, Alice's life has been very structured; now her life shifts; it becomes fragmented until it ends with a nightmarish awakening. Throughout the novel, Alice is filled with unconscious feelings of morbidity, physical disgrace, unfairness, and bizarre feelings about bodily functions. Everywhere there is the absurd, unexplainable notion of death and the absolute meaninglessness of death and life.

Alice's final triumph occurs when she outgrows nonsense. In response to the Queen's cry at the Knave's trial: "sentence first — verdict afterward," Alice responds: "Stuff and nonsense! Who cares for *you?* You're nothing but a pack of cards!" At last, Alice takes control of her life and her growth toward maturity by shattering and scattering the absurdity of the playing cards and the silly little creatures who are less rational than she is. In waking from her nightmare, she realizes that reason *can* oppose nonsense, and that it can — and did — win. And now that the dream of chaos is over, she can say, from her distance above-ground, "It *was* a curious dream," but then she skips off thinking that — for a strange moment — what a wonderful dream it was.

SUMMARIES AND COMMENTARIES

CHAPTER I

"Down the Rabbit-Hole"

Alice in Wonderland begins as a pleasant fairy tale. Alice and her sister are reading a book that has neither pictures nor conversations. Alice finds the reading tedious; she is anxious for more vivid and direct forms of experience. Her boredom and anxiety cause her to withdraw from the "civilized pastime" of reading dull books and to fall to sleep, entering the world of dreams. At the edge of semi-sleep consciousness, she sees the form of a white rabbit scurrying toward a rabbit-hole. Immediately, Alice is curious and pursues him down the hole. The reason for Alice's pursuit is that she burns with curiosity; after all, the rabbit is wearing a waistcoat, talking to himself, walking upright, and he has a pocket watch; his image is thus unusual, suggesting romantic and fairy tale "people." The rabbit's hole functions like a large laundry chute, and, curiously, Alice "floats" down the hole in a slow descent. In her fall, she has fantasies relating to the absence of gravity, the quality of infinite space, the shape of her body, mass, and velocity. Her free, fanciful associations in the tunnel are in vivid contrast to her innocent, non-reflective curiosity that led her to leap down the hole in the first place.

In fact, her leap downward probably was unconscious. Not once did she hesitate for fear of what she might find or consider how she might get out. Her leap was a leap in a spirit of adventure, a reckless gamble done for fun.

On the other hand, Alice retains her belief in the world aboveground. There are shelves lining the walls of the tunnel, and on one shelf she finds a jar of orange marmalade. Things like the jar (which is empty) reaffirm her feelings that matters are not "too different" here, so she refuses to accept that her experience of floating down a rabbit-hole is unlike previous, curious adventures that she has had. This is just another adventure, and fancying that she might well be headed through the earth's center, she wonders how to determine her latitude and longitude. Note that it doesn't seem to matter to her that such terms do not apply *under* the earth's surface. Then, Alice considers the prospect of emerging head downward in New Zealand or Australia; her concern is almost a caricature of her childish belief in the impossible.

Strangely enough, there is no indication that she is truly disoriented; everything seems true to sense in spite of the absence of acceleration and gravity. Even her "sense of propriety" is functioning. She returns the empty marmalade jar to a lower shelf for fear that to drop it might injure someone below. Then, in an imaginary conversation with a woman whom she might meet on the other side of the world, she manages to curtsy in mid-air. Yet, already she is beginning to suffer nostalgia for her life in the conscious, above-ground world. The frightening possibility of being trapped in a dream occurs to her. Above-ground, her cat Dinah had an appetite for bats, and Alice is suddenly confronted by the thought that, possibly, *bats may also eat cats!* The age-old questions of eating, or being eaten, poses itself here in the context of an alien world while Alice is falling, falling . . . to heaven knows where.

Wonderland is one of the most spontaneous "places" in this novel. And suddenly Alice is in Wonderland! She has landed safely at the bottom of her long, slow fall. But, immediately, she hears the White Rabbit's anxious lament: "Oh, my ears and whiskers, how late it's getting!" Alice then loses sight of the rabbit in a hall that is paneled with doors. None of them, however, seems to be the right size for even a young girl of Alice's size; in fact, they are "strange doors." They seem to have a foreboding, funereal feeling about them. Thus, she does not attempt to open them.

On a glass table, though, she finds a tiny golden key, and this key opens a small, curtained door; but the entrance-way is small, rat-sized, in fact, and Alice cannot fit even her head through the doorway. And the door leads to a beautifully colorful, seemingly "enchanted garden." Alice wishes so very much that she could reduce her size and could explore the garden. Her wish that she could reverse her size is consistent with the logic of fantasy. Already, as the narrator observes, ". . . so many out-of-the-way things had happened lately, that Alice had begun to think that few things indeed were really impossible."

On the glass table, Alice finds a little bottle. It seems to have just magically appeared. The label on the bottle reads "DRINK ME." It is against her previous, proper English training to eat or drink strange foods, but curiosity (she *is* a child, after all) proves a stronger compulsion than doing the "right thing." So she drinks the liquid and is reduced immediately; now she can pass through the doorway leading to the garden! *But* she forgot to take the key before she drank the liquid, and now she has shrunk down to a tiny little girl. Disheartened that she can no longer reach the key, Alice begins to cry.

Then there is a curious change in her attitude. She stops herself from crying, as though her "selfish self" has been detached from her "proper self" and the latter is scolding her for crying. We almost hear her mother's voice: a desire for something *right now* is childish; it is "narcissistic" — selfish. It is naughty, and little girls shouldn't be selfish and want things *right now*. Thus, Alice restrains herself from crying. Suddenly, a little glass box appears with a cake inside it (this is underneath the three-legged table). On the cake, there is a sign: "EAT ME." Alice eats the cake, but there is no *immediate* consequence. To her dismay, life is dull once again; it seems as though she has not really left the above-ground world at all. She feels that she is the same frustrated little girl that she was before. Except now there's an additional problem. When she was a normal-sized girl, she could not get out of the passageway, and now that she is too small, she has no means to escape. So there she sits, an enclosed soul, trapped in the traumatic nightmare of a prison cell. Already logic has begun to break down in this confusing, claustrophobic condition. Life is beginning to become exaggerated. Alice feels that she can't trust her sanity; curiosity seems to have taken its place. Thus, here in this introduction, rational expectations have taken Alice to an illogical and fantastic destination.

CHAPTER II

"The Pool of Tears"

As things turn out, the magic cake has a delayed effect. Suddenly, Alice's neck shoots up like a telescope, unfurling until her head touches the ceiling. "Curiouser and curiouser!" she exclaims. But that is all she says; she isn't angry, and her ungrammatical outburst is merely indicative of her being a surprised child. Her emotion is one of awe. That is all, and it shows her inherent self-control. However, she clearly realizes again that a serious problem is going to be her new *size*. And because *size* is related to what one eats or drinks, her concern is to eat and drink properly, but that seems almost impossible down here. One can't *trust* what one reads on little signs.

Note that the extension of Alice's neck has had an inverse effect on the other limbs of her body. Her arms now appear to be small stumps, her head seems miniscule, and, without relatively-sized shoulders or hips, her trunk resembles a frame minus any curves. In the John Tenniel illustrations (as many critics have noted), Alice appears almost phallic looking, much like a totem figure. But whatever the connotations imply about Lewis Carroll's fantasies, they are certainly unknown to Alice. Nothing in the story suggests that the pre-pubescent heroine has any self-consciousness about her oddly elongated, phallic-looking neck.

If Alice has any serious hangup at this point, it is related to food, because *food* always seems to produce trouble. Whenever Alice eats something, she becomes alienated from her body and her sense of who she is. After eating the cake, she wonders how amusing it will be to communicate by mail with her *feet!* Carroll is a master at reproducing the curiosity that can only surface in dreams. This is a child's world of the Absurd, and Alice is speculating on *possibilities.* Then, her Victorian training checks her whimsy: "Oh dear, what nonsense I'm talking!"

In despair again because the "proper" and rational side of her has come to the fore, Alice begins to cry, and again her "super-ego" – the voice of Authority – intervenes: "You ought to be ashamed of yourself, a great girl like you . . . to go on crying in this way! Stop this moment, I tell you!"

There is often this two-voiced sense of herself in Alice's soliloquies; there is the sense of propriety, as well as the voice of a separate child-self which keeps emerging, the latter growing stronger and stronger. It is the voice of a slowly, gradually maturing Alice as she becomes more adult, but note that she is very much "her own" adult as the story unfolds. At this point, of course, Alice is not aware that this shifting identity is a problem. That awareness will come later, after many more confrontations in Wonderland.

The humor that manifests itself in her talks to herself is mainly produced by her solemn attitude, when compared to her child's attitude and reaction to whatever queer situation she finds herself in. In spite of what has happened to Alice, she tries very hard to be totally serious about it and to *try* and make sense out of all this *nonsense.* Nonetheless, the laugh is on her, for the narrator's third-person voice always plays up Alice's child-like, comic aspects. He makes Alice's credibility at *trying* to be rational – despite her deep curiosity – ridiculous. This, of course, is the core of Carroll's humor in the novel.

One consequence of this two-voice structure is that Alice has no terribly strong emotions either way; her responses to the creatures in Wonderland seem totally cerebral. But she *tries*, as we have said, to deal with them as though they were logical and thinking beings – even though they are "creatures" and although they make no sense at all.

Alice forms no lasting relationships with any of them. In fact, in the climactic last chapter, she displays inflamed anger toward the Queen of Hearts; her only real expression of sympathy is for the Knave of Hearts.

As French philosopher Henri Bergson once observed, laughter and emotions are incompatible – which is perhaps why jokes by people who laugh while telling them are seldom as funny as jokes told without expression or those which are told with deadpan expressions. And inasmuch as the mad creatures of Wonderland never laugh or ever seem amused (not even, really, the Cheshire-Cat), the comic effect of Alice's dream becomes highly enhanced – that is, the story becomes funnier to the reader, even though at times it must seem scary to a child. But when the creatures are the saddest (the Mock Turtle, for example), or anxious (the White Rabbit), or enraged (the Queen of Hearts), or frightened (the gardeners), they seem all the more amusing and comic.

The parenthetical comments that the narrator sometimes inserts into the text greatly assist the graphic relationship between comedy and horror. The style and tone of the narrative is usually lucid, calm, a bit condescending, even snobbish at times, but it is also loving and indulgent. And then at other times, it is distant and hostile. The writing in *Alice in Wonderland*, you should note, is *always* on the edge of hysteria. So intense is it, that the split between man and nature is implicit in all of Alice's encounters with the creatures in Wonderland.

Part of the humor of cruelty – and the creatures of Wonderland are sometimes extremely cruel – is to maintain the balance between sadism and sentimentality. In this case, the split effect provides a proper tension and gives the writing a subtlety and a sober delicacy.

The double consciousness in the character of Alice is also a structural motif – a duality reflecting Alice's regression, at times, to a small child, and then a reversal, when she becomes a stern, Victorian moralist. At times, Alice's willfulness provides an escape from boredom. It irritates her to be corrected by creatures who sound irrational. Then, at other times, she wants to sink into the ground.

Here, Carroll sharpens the opposition of the two opposing impulses within Alice. Later, even Alice realizes that part of herself scolds and is very much like the critical creatures who live in Wonderland. Her search for true feeling and for some sanity in this strange world turns finally inward toward maturity, knowledge, and self-awareness, although she herself would (and will) not realize anything about herself unless it is involved in some sort of *external* experience. In order to know her true inner feelings, Alice will have to finally educate that other "scolding" Alice-voice which is confused by her estranged condition and trying always to cope with it *rationally.*

Alice cries until she is sitting in – what is to her – a gigantic pool of tears, even though in reality, the pool is only four inches deep. The White Rabbit reappears, bewailing his reception by the savage Duchess. Alice, with her long neck, startles him so that he drops his fan and gloves and scurries off.

Taking up the fan and gloves, Alice says: "Dear, dear! How queer everything is today!" Amid the fun, Alice is beginning to recognize something ominous; therefore, it is only natural that she tries to relate her present situation ("today") to the rigid, secure "order" of the past. She leapt down the rabbit-hole without any thought of how she would get out, and now her adventure has already begun to fragment her old structure of living a rather ordinary, boring, uninteresting day-to-day life. This disorientation is very much like a jarring fall – which she would have had if she had *actually* fallen down a truly deep hole. Her old world is collapsing fast. She must simultaneously attempt to discover how to begin to understand her dream while, at the same time, try to determine how it will *end.* She attempts to re-establish her identity by asking herself if she could have become *some other child.* But her sensibility as a proper Victorian little girl and also as an intelligent, educated middle-class girl make her dismiss any of the children who come to mind. "I'm sure I can't be Mabel, for I know all sorts of things, and she, oh, she knows such a very little." Nor is Alice helped in trying to figure out who she is by recalling logical certainties – such as arithmetic. When she attempts to establish who she is by reciting her multiplication tables from one to twenty, her uncertainty only deepens: "Let me see: four times five is twelve, and four times six is thirteen, and four times seven is – oh dear! I shall never get to twenty at that rate!"

Alice finds her distress unrelieved. She has no resources to help her. Wonderland is one enormous puzzle, and her solitude and alienation have now made her unsure whether or not *she* really exists as *Alice!* Her familiar, comforting world of facts and learning are no longer mentally true, and she wishes desperately for people whom she left behind to relieve her boredom. She knows that "It'll be no use their putting their heads down and saying 'Come up again, dear!' I shall only look up and say, 'Who am I, then? Tell me that first, and then, if I like being that person, I'll come up: if not, I'll stay down here till I'm somebody else.' "

The most crucial aspect of her sanity—her permanent self-identity—seems destroyed. But her lonely cry does express her horrible loneliness: "I do wish they *would* put their heads down! I am so very tired of being all alone here!"

All this while, Alice has been fanning herself and has put on one of the White Rabbit's gloves. Suddenly, she realizes that she has *shrunk*—and is *continuing to shrink!* In alarm, she drops the fan, and the shrinking stops. She realizes in horror that she might well have vanished into thin air if she had held the fan much longer.

As we have already noted, her trials have a serial nature, for no sooner has she stopped shrinking than she finds herself floating in the pool of her own tears. This is like a non-stop movie of horrors! In a single moment, she has passed from the threat of *vanishing,* and now she faces the prospect of *drowning.*

Some critics have interpreted her sea of tears as a symbolic evocation of a Lethean bath from which Alice will emerge "reborn." But Alice does not change. She swims and frolics until she is joined by a Mouse. His appearance enables Carroll to now parody one of the Victorians' favorite pastimes in which they educated their children: by rote learning.

In a soliloquy, Alice addresses the Mouse: "Oh Mouse," a phrase which reminds her instantly of a Latin grammar exercise in her brother's Latin textbook: *amo, amas, amat.* Then she recalls the English translation rather than the Latin conjugation of the verb for *love,* and what follows is a confusing of a *noun* declension: "A mouse—of a mouse—to a mouse—a mouse—O mouse!"

All of this is absolute nonsense to the Mouse, and Alice's attempt at further communication with the Mouse becomes further complicated when she tries to converse with the Mouse in French. Tactlessly, she chooses the phrase *"Ou est ma chatte?"* Of course, absurdly, the Mouse understands "cat" (*chatte*) in *any* language, and his initial apprehension of Alice quickly turns to fear and distrust. He swims away, very offended and very discomforted. Alice then realizes her blunder, but she keeps blathering away, describing her cat, Dinah. Alice is clearly out of control. And when she does fully realize the extent of her offense, she tries to switch the subject to *dogs* – as if dogs might make the Mouse feel any better. Her tactless bungling then becomes a predominating pattern. Nonetheless, the Mouse offers to tell her his history and why he dislikes cats *and* dogs, and he forgives her. Curiously, his maturity and politeness is in sharp contrast with Alice's unthinking, cruel lapse of manners. Alice is redeemed here only by the Mouse's having an adult sensibility. He forgives Alice because, as a child, she does not know any better. Chapter II concludes, then, with the pool of tears becoming suddenly filled with a strange menagerie of Wonderland creatures: a Duck, a Dodo, a Lory (a parrot), an Eaglet, and "several other curious creatures."

CHAPTER III

"A Caucus-Race and a Long Tale"

"How to dry off" is the central concern at the beginning of this chapter. Alice finds herself embroiled in a heated discussion with the Lory (the parrot) over who knows best how to dry off. The Lory cuts off the argument with the declaration that *he* is wiser than Alice because he is *older* than she is. In this dispute Alice becomes a child again – therefore, sort of an underdog – but her self-centered emotions indicate a mental maturity well beyond her chronological age. Still, in relation to the other animals, Alice seems altogether like the dependent child that she really is; but clearly the Lory's rude position reflects that although he *may* be more mature, *we* don't know that he is necessarily older than Alice. In any case, Alice will not let the Lory's response go unchallenged, and the scene turns hilarious when the Lory absolutely refuses to reveal his true age.

All along, the Mouse has seemed to assume himself to be the natural "authority figure" of this motley group, so he offers "to dry" the creatures by telling them a dry history. The Mouse states that ". . . the Patriotic Archbishop of Canterbury found it advisable . . ." but before he finishes, the Duck interrupts: "Found what?"

"Found it," the Mouse replies rather crossly, adding, "Of course you know what *it* means."

Wonderland certainly demands a strange "consistency" (one can't say 'logic') of its own – especially concerning language, for like the Eaglet's "Speak English!" the language of ordinary discourse is ambiguous. The Mouse's "it" could, of course, mean absolutely *anything*. At any rate, the dull, dry history of England does *not* help "dry" anyone. So the Dodo (an extinct bird) proposes a Caucus-race. Alice asks the Dodo to explain the Caucus-race, and he replies that "the best way to explain it is to do it." The Eaglet challenges him to "Speak English!" Thus, the Dodo explains that he is proposing that the creatures dry themselves in a race in which everyone starts and stops running when and where they please, and all win the race. For an extinct creature, the Dodo has a curious sport: natural selection, the cause of his extinction, is a race in which only the best win.

Alice thinks that the Caucus-race is absurd, but she participates in the running anyway. As an indication that the other animals recognize her superiority, she is selected to bestow the prizes (comfits, or candy, from her pockets). After the candy is distributed, however, *she* remains without a prize. The Dodo then suggests that she be rewarded with the only thing left in her pocket, an elegant thimble, which he gives to her as *her* prize.

The Caucus-race, of course, satirizes all political caucuses and the wheeling and dealing of politics in which, to win an election, a politician often has to ensure that even his opponents feel that they all have won *something* with the victor's win. Certainly a prize to everyone does lessen the rise of jealousies and rivalries, but Alice wants to laugh, and the gravity of the other creatures intimidates her. Her amusement reflects a Victorian Tory of the nineteenth century; political progress at that time was essentially random and circular, a sentiment best summarized in the French saying: *Plus ca change, plus c'est la même chose* (or in English: the more things change, the more they stay the same).

Having discovered that the Mouse has bitter memories of his enemies, Alice asks him to tell the history he promised. But rather than a personal autobiography, however, the Mouse's story is a genetic-racial memory. On the printed page, his "tale" resembles a sprawling, elongated (and the print becomes tinier and tinier) mouse's tail. It is a brutal story of an encounter between a mouse and a dog ("Fury") in a house. The story ends with the dog executing the mouse after a trial. The Mouse's sad tale prefigures the entire plot of *Alice in Wonderland*, for Alice will finally dispose of all of Wonderland because of her anger at the injustice of the Knave of Hearts' trial.

The calligrammatic tale/tail teaches Alice nothing about the Mouse's past experiences, so after the Mouse departs in a rage, Alice goofs again. This time, she offends the Canary and the Magpie by describing Dinah's appetite for birds. Leaving her judgment about "what *is* safe to talk about" in limbo, she abandons her basic sensitivity; it simply can't be trusted here in this strange world of Wonderland. Her existence here is certainly becoming "curiouser and curiouser" because she cannot identify with the other creatures and their natures. On the other hand, her subversive (so the creatures think) attempt at communication is collapsing into mad, slapstick kinds of verbal play. Not only does Wonderland's language have a false logic, but the very definition of terms rests upon inconsistencies. In fact, so consistent are the illogicalities that nonsense appears to be the "norm" and the basis of Wonderland.

CHAPTER IV

"The Rabbit Sends in a Little Bill"

In a dramatic, magical shift, Alice suddenly finds herself in the presence of the White Rabbit. But the glass table and the great hall have vanished. There is a clear contrast between the calmness of Alice and the nervous, agitated White Rabbit, looking frantically for his lost fan and gloves. Typically, however, the White Rabbit is *always* fretting over his appearance *and* the time, while Alice's problem concerns her physical size changes and her identity crisis. In a way, the two characters embody concerns of youth and age. For youth, the question is to establish an identity; for an older person, there is usually a constant wish to have the appearance, at least, of an identity, and there is usually a "fretting" about time, since one is more and more aware of the little time left for living as each day passes.

Alice's central problem in this chapter is accentuated very suddenly. The White Rabbit mistakes her for his house servant, Mary Ann, and he orders her to fetch a spare pair of gloves and fan at his house. His air of authority makes her obey him even though she resents her new status: "How queer it seems to be going on messages for a rabbit! I suppose Dinah'll be sending me on messages next!" Alice clearly knows the difference between herself and *servants*. But in Wonderland's bewildering anarchy, she is forever *trying* to make sense and order — in social status. It is her very Victorian class-consciousness that makes her reasonable, self-controlled and polite; yet her sense of class also makes her resent the creatures' nasty, insulting treatment. Class, in the end, distinguishes Alice from the eccentric creatures of Wonderland; whereas she always seems reserved, they seem ever at the mercy of their whims; and they are usually either ill-mannered, or grotesquely inept (the Mouse, for example).

At the White Rabbit's house, Alice finds the fan and the rabbit's gloves, and yet she is seemingly, uncontrollably drawn again to yet another bottle labeled "DRINK ME." She takes a nip of the liquid, and suddenly she is too large to leave the room; again, her curiosity and appetite have gotten her into trouble. However, this is no longer just "curious": growing too large is becoming a nightmarish theme; in this instance, Alice's growing larger—and then smaller—form a sort of internal rhythm that most children connect with time—that is, sometimes time *seems* long; sometimes, it seems short. Yet the consequences of eating or drinking the wrong things never result—in the real world—in one's becoming suddenly very wee or truly gigantic. Alice's size here brings her to regret her adventure: "It was much pleasanter at home," she thinks. Seemingly, she has "grown up," something she has long wanted to do; but now she laments the fact that growing up has not made her any more of an adult: "Shall I *never* get any older than I am now?" She's very big, but she's still a child. "Well, that'll be a comfort, one way—never to be an old woman—but then—always to have lessons to learn!"

The White Rabbit, meanwhile, has lost his patience and followed Alice to his house. He is in a furious mood, which frightens Alice, so she prevents him from entering the house. The humor here is due to the fact of Alice's being many, many times larger than the rabbit and, logically, she should have no reason at all to fear him. Nonetheless, the White Rabbit's angry, brusque orders are terribly intimidating to her because the White Rabbit *sounds* like an adult. For Alice (a well-trained child), no matter how impolite an adult is, an adult must be minded and must be feared. Adults may be a puzzle (and rude) but, to a child, their domination must be accepted *at all times.* Alice's real world society, then, is responsible for her behavior here and is further enforced by her class consciousness.

Prevented from entering his own house, the White Rabbit calls to his gardener, Pat. Here, note that whereas the White Rabbit speaks in standard, formal English, Pat has an Irish brogue (as does Bill the Lizard and the "card gardeners" in the "enchanted garden"). Pat recommends that "little" Bill (see chapter title) the Lizard enter the house through the chimney and evict Alice; because of his shape, Bill should have no trouble squeezing down the chimney. So Bill goes down the chimney, but Alice kicks him fiercely back *up* the chimney as soon as he reaches the fireplace.

Suddenly, there is a heavy, claustrophobic feeling within Alice, but she is by no means helpless. In contrast, it is the "tiny creatures" who are truly frustrated, and we see now a direct basis for Alice's disillusionment with "growing up." At last, she is physically large enough to control Wonderland's creatures, but she is unable to do so because her enormous size has her trapped in the rabbit's small house.

Without warning, the irate White Rabbit and his servants begin pelting Alice with small pebbles. More trouble! But as the pebbles land on the floor, they magically turn into *cakes!* Remembering that cakes had previously had an opposite effect to liquid, Alice eats a cake and is suddenly small again. Then, however, the creatures outside promptly attack her and chase her off.

Alice is now so small that she has to hide; all the creatures whom she sees are loathsome, especially a "monstrous" puppy, which nearly crushes her. In Alice's words, the puppy is "a dear little puppy" but because of his size, he might as well be "the villainous Fury" of the Mouse's tale. Alice does her best to escape from the puppy because since he is so big and she is so small, she is in just exactly the kind of jeopardy that the Mouse described. The puppy, friendly as he seems to large adults, is a brute to Alice, and the life of a tiny little Alice is certainly of no consequence to him. This impression is strengthened by the puppy's constant delight in almost trampling on her.

After she escapes from the puppy, Alice finds herself under a large mushroom, and on top of the mushroom sits a large blue caterpillar smoking a water-pipe (a "hookah").

CHAPTER V

"Advice from a Caterpillar"

Alice is well acquainted by now with the prime principle of Wonderland's chaos: illogic. Yet she continues – almost by instinct – to oppose the illogical context in which she continually finds herself.

Yet her experience so far should have prepared her for the possibility that the "pebble-cake" might *not* have reduced her size. But as eating cake *had* worked that way once before, she expected (logically) the same results. And, indeed, the cake produced the desired effect. Thus, it is the *reader* who is surprised!

Nothing has really changed, though. All of Alice's moral precepts – order, the idea and the use of logic, and precise language – have become turned upside-down; they are now either meaningless concepts, or cruel and twisted confusions for her. In her encounter with the blue Caterpillar, for example, the destruction of her identity and her belief in ordinary language, social manners, and human superiority to animals is intensified.

"Who are you?" the Caterpillar asks her. Alice replies in a negative, defensive, and tentative way: "I – I hardly know, Sir, just at present – at least I know who I *was* when I got up this morning, but I think I must have been changed several times since then."

The way that Alice responds to the Caterpillar is as significant as what she says. Compared to the other creatures that she has met, the Caterpillar is downright nasty. For him, all conventions of social etiquette have been cast away. Alice's attempts to display respect and politeness – by addressing him as "Sir" simply produce harsh derision and scorn. And he becomes even ruder – to the point of provocation. This is all becoming horribly frustrating! The conventions of social etiquette all seem to be working against Alice, and she has no recourse. She has no other set of standards or values. All of her training has conditioned her to simply bear impoliteness with politeness. It is *not* easy.

The crudity of the Caterpillar's first question is emphasized by the narrator's remark that such a question was not easy for Alice to answer. In the context of the dialogue, the narrator's voice reveals a wry touch of humor. But given what Alice has just been through, the haughty question is hardly a humorous one. The question "Who are you?" can be very hostile – especially when one is addressed by a *blue* Caterpillar. His cold and snide observations reduce Alice's feelings to a pathetic, suppressed anger. When he repeats his nasty question, she says in a grave, but exasperated voice: "I think you ought to tell me who you are first." In a devastating retort, the Caterpillar says: "Why?"

It is obvious that such an exchange imposes upon Alice simply more insecurity and feelings of guilt. Yet those kinds of feelings cannot be sustained for long; all too quickly they become hostile and negative. It is all Alice can do to contain her anger. The strength of her repressed feelings is a bit amusing to the reader. Her deliberate, determined restraint reveals the secret of much of the story's tension. Her self-control is remarkably exaggerated because Alice is a "proper little girl."

The Caterpillar's attitude has so frustrated her that Alice turns to leave him, but he pleads with her to come back, and after she reluctantly does, he says: "Keep your temper."

"Is that all?" asks Alice, more angry than ever.

The Caterpillar then further outrages her. He asks her how she thinks she has *changed*. Alice tells him that she can't remember things and that her size is *always* changing. Earlier, when she attempted to recite the very Victorian, very moralistic poem "How Doth the Little Busy Bee," for instance, "it all came different." In a deceptively simple form of mistranslation, Alice made a dutiful creature (the bee) become a slothful creature (a crocodile). The poem she mangles here is very much akin to what happened in Chapter II, for in that poem she kept saying: "How doth the little crocodile" – an animal who grins and eats little fish that swim into his mouth.

Carroll's parody of "proper" Victorian, didactic children's verses continues with the Caterpillar commanding her to recite "You Are Old, Father William." But the Father William poem comes out just as *immoral* and just as *altered* as the crocodile/bee poem. Each subject becomes the antithesis of the correct "moral" of the "correct verse." The Caterpillar tells Alice that her recitation is wrong because it is *totally* against the intent of "the true originals." Of course, it is – and that's what frustrates Alice so. Instead of being an old man of moderate pleasures, Father William is a lusty, scheming hedonist: he advises his son that the secret of longevity and health is an active, self-indulgent life – the very *opposite* of conventional wisdom on how to reach a ripe old, proper Victorian age.

At the conclusion of Alice's verse recital, the two mutually antagonistic temperaments move to a final clash. We almost see Alice gnashing her teeth in frustration as she tells the Caterpillar that she wishes she were larger than just *three* inches tall. Naturally, the Caterpillar is offended by the implication that there is something wrong with being three inches tall – since that is exactly *his height* when he is extended on his tail.

Thus, he explodes in anger and becomes viciously insulting. Then he abruptly crawls away in a huff. Once more, we are reminded of the unceasing antipathy between Alice and the creatures of Wonderland.

Oddly enough, in spite of the blue Caterpillar's anger, before he leaves Alice, he gives her the secret of realizing her wish. As he exits, he remarks: "One side [of the mushroom] will make you grow taller, and the other side will make you grow shorter." Perplexed, Alice asks *herself*: "One side of what?" The clairvoyant Caterpillar says: "Of the mushroom"—just as if she had asked the question aloud. Note that neither Alice nor the Caterpillar acts as though this act of mind-reading is anything extraordinary. Each of them seems to accept mind-reading as a matter of course. Alice has obviously been so thoroughly exasperated by the bizarre shrinkages and physical distortions inflicted upon her throughout the day that the Caterpillar's mental feat no longer impresses her. If she can converse at all with a Caterpillar, his mind-reading can't be much more extraordinary. But, remember, the creatures of Wonderland *never* behave as though they are abnormal.

The mushroom has predictable effects. This time, it leaves Alice with a curving, serpentine neck. There is a curious irony at play here: the Caterpillar again provides Alice with the means of changing her *size* rather than simply, psychologically, "growing up." Caterpillars, of course, emerge from a chrysalis as newborn butterflies or moths; they die, so to speak, to be reborn. Alice, however, never experiences a similar metamorphosis. In fact, she resents any notion that she is anyone other than who she has *always* been.

A good case here can be made that part of her objection to "growing up" is based on her fear of losing her identity. So long as she remains young Alice, she is innocent of good and evil. But with her neck suddenly slithering through the tree branches, she appears to be the embodiment of evil. In fact, a pigeon-hen immediately thinks that Alice is an egg-eating snake.

Thus, the Pigeon's attack on Alice changes Wonderland from a pastoral garden to a primal jungle of violence and death. Alice denies that she is a serpent. "I—I'm a little girl," she says, remembering the number of changes she has gone through during the day. "A likely story indeed!" smirks the Pigeon.

Alice is again unable to triumph at the cost of an "adult." On the contrary, she feels compelled to assume a role as it is defined for her by others, and the Pigeon, once more, reinforces Alice's problem of identity. Like her series of size changes, Alice's entire existence is one gigantic question mark. Her problem is that she truly sympathizes with the Pigeon's desire to protect the nest. Nevertheless, Alice fears that she won't be able to *prove* that she is, truly, just a little girl with an extremely long neck. And the Pigeon rejects Alice's claim—especially after she admits that Yes, she *has* eaten eggs. But her protests that she has no designs on these particular eggs come to nothing, and the Pigeon vehemently orders her away from the nest.

In a state of rejection, Alice desperately tries to reduce herself back to her previous size. She still has some of the Caterpillar's mushroom, so she nibbles at pieces of it, and by a process of trial and error, she begins to be able to control her size. Thus, her success in using the mushroom to obtain the desired height shows how well she is beginning to apply the logic of size reversibility.

CHAPTER VI

"Pig and Pepper"

The Caterpillar's nasty mood, even if he does *seem* nonchalant, is a subtle symbol of all the verbal chaos in Wonderland. Yet, here, in Chapter VI, that linguistic nonsense is replaced by random, violent, *physical disorder* in the action of the story.

Alice has come upon a house, just as a Fish-Footman delivers a letter to the Frog-Footman of the house. The letter is an invitation, which the Fish-Footman reads: "For the Duchess. An invitation from the Queen to play croquet." In a marvelous example of Wonderland's semantic, verbal fun, the Frog-Footman reverses the invitation: "From the Queen. An invitation for the Duchess to play croquet." In reality, it should *end* with "From the Queen."

When Alice attempts to enter the house, she finds herself further into the world of nonsense. The Frog-Footman is sitting before the door and is totally *un*cooperative as she knocks at the door. He replies to her every question in "absurd" reasoning—as if Alice had suddenly found herself in a Samuel Beckett play. With elegant precision, the Frog-Footman explains that her knocking on the door is useless because he can only answer the door from inside. Again, we see an illustration where the reply to a question is never addressed *to* the question, but to something else. Alice's knocking on the door is "useless," she is told, because the Frog-Footman, who opens the door from inside the house, is now *outside*; thus, he can't answer her; and, in any event, the noise from *inside* the house would prevent the Frog-Footman from hearing her knock *even if* he were inside. Truly, this *is* the World of the Absurd.

Yet, this kind of confusion is quite normal in Wonderland; *all* of reality here is viewed, so to speak, on a scale of values which are completely alien to the "normal" Victorian world of Alice.

A large plate suddenly comes flying out of the house and barely misses hitting the Frog-Footman's head. The Frog-Footman is totally oblivious to this. And his indifference to chaos is characteristic of Wonderland's creatures and indicates to Alice that there surely must be an underlying order here. Or perhaps it involves only a fatalistic indifference. For the Caterpillar and the Frog-Footman, things have *no purpose*. "I shall sit here," the Frog-Footman muses, "on and off for days and days."

"But what am I to do?" asks Alice.

"Anything you like," says the Frog-Footman.

The Frog-Footman's reply to Alice's question is idiotic nonsense, and with a child's simplicity, Alice finds the Frog-Footman's values totally illogical. Alice has been brought up to believe that things should be done and that they should be done with a purpose. In her world, there is order and there are schedules and tasks to be accomplished at certain times. Carroll's method in creating the tension between these two worlds is to increase the difference in the values "above-ground" and those of Wonderland. One is, therefore, not entirely correct in relating Wonderland's anarchy and nonsense to the creatures' irrational behavior. Alice, in fact, is making the assumption that there is — and *should be* — an order here; she is trying to make logic from illogic. Wonderland is a world of illogic, and Alice, as a proper little Victorian girl, keeps trying throughout the novel to relate, logically, to these creatures — who *seem* like adults and who, therefore, should be logical.

The creatures' acceptance of disorder may seem to be a parody of reality to the reader. Yet Wonderland's chaos is not altogether unreal. Our own reality, as a historical one, is impermanent and never without some degree of ambiguity. When we consider what has been accepted as "reality" throughout the ages regarding our world and its place in the Order of Things, we see how flimsy a word "logic" can be. Indeed, Alfred Einstein, the father of relativity, was deeply worried that God was "playing dice with the universe." If Alice fails to discover a correlation between her reality above-ground and her dream, it must be because she is "inside" her dream. To put it another way, one might even say that she is trapped in an unadjustable frame of meaning. For her, there is no scale of values except the one which she brings to Wonderland. She has a strong sense of being lost and abandoned; but the *creatures* know where *they* belong, and *none* of them identifies with her plight. Nor are the creatures able to befriend her. Note that Alice meets *no other children like herself* in Wonderland. And the creatures all speak to her on the inscrutable and mysterious level of adults. Unless they direct her to do something, their utterances are quite beyond her comprehension. In that sense, in Alice's dream, they are echoing memories of the many puzzling things that adults living above-ground have said, things that Alice did not understand.

Inside the house, Alice meets the Duchess, who nurses a crying baby. A cook, meanwhile, stirs a cauldron of soup and, indiscriminately, she shakes a pepper mill. The baby is crying, and it is sneezing, it seems, because of all the flying pepper. Next to the cook sits the Cheshire-Cat with his famous smile. The kitchen is in an absolute turmoil. But the Duchess ignores the sneezing, the crying, and the cook throwing pans. Alice watches silently as the Duchess brutally shakes and pounds the baby. The Duchess' rudeness and cruelty is the most extreme thus far in the story; even the cook is provoked to the point of directing her pans at the Duchess. Calmly, the Duchess ignores the others' reactions.

"If everybody minded their business," the Duchess says, "the world would go around a deal faster than it does."

"Which would not be an advantage," observes Alice.

"Talking of axes," says the Duchess, "Chop off her head!" The Duchess is abominable, and the baby bears the worst of her cruelty. While violently throwing the baby around, the Duchess sings a crude and savage lullaby:

> Speak roughly to your little boy,
> And beat him when he sneezes:
> He only does it to annoy,
> Because he knows it teases.

The cook and the baby then recite a chorus to each stanza:

"Wow! wow! wow!"

This verse, like the others before it, is another parody of a well-known poem in Carroll's time. Alice is rightly appalled at the lullaby's sentiments and the Duchess' cruelty. Every now and then, the Duchess calls the baby "Pig!" This is proof enough that the Duchess has a barbarous nature.

As the Duchess prepares to go play croquet with the Queen, she tosses the baby to Alice. Suddenly, Alice feels maternal and thinks that she must save the baby from the violent Duchess and from the crazy cook. But in the next moment, Alice finds that her sympathy is falsely placed. The baby struggles to get out of her embrace, and before Alice's very eyes, the baby is transformed into a grunting pig.

Confident that she *was* doing the right thing—despite the metamorphosis that is happening before her very eyes—Alice still finds her good intentions subverted by Wonderland's absurdities. Finally, she has no choice but to let the pig trot off, but she cannot let it go without a twinge of guilt. She considers it a handsome pig—but an *ugly baby.* Implicit in this observation is the assumption that "all things have a silver lining," a very Victorian type of thought. Alice remembers children who "might do well as pigs . . . if one only knew the right way to change them."

Alice has a new sense of self-satisfaction and superiority that has been reinforced by the contemptible behavior of the Duchess. She "saved" the pig/baby. Indeed, in the face of the rudeness she has experienced, Alice is finding that she doesn't have to struggle so hard to remain a "lady." All she has to do is *not* react to the crazy provocation that she meets. But even so, her moral superiority illustrates her painful isolation, and not even the smiling Cheshire-Cat enables her to relax for very long, for despite his wonderfully large smile, the cat has "long claws and a great many teeth."

Just after the pig trots away, Alice notices the Cheshire-Cat sitting on a bough in a tree. Whereas the Duchess is unpleasant and threatening, the friendly Cheshire-Cat treats Alice with a measure of respect—though he is no less maddening in his response to her questions. The Cat is neither didactic nor hostile; still, he is no less inconsistent. If he doesn't snap at her, he *still confuses* her. Seemingly, he is an honest cat, but Alice cannot make sense of his "honesty." For example, when Alice asks him which way to go, he responds: "That depends a good deal on where you want to get to." As Alice responds that she doesn't care, he replies: "Then it doesn't matter which way you go." He assures her that she will get somewhere if she only walks long enough; she is sure to reach the same destination regardless of the direction that she takes. Unlike the other creatures, the Cheshire-Cat *does* seem fair. However, he too creates frustration within Alice in exactly the very same illogical ways that adults have so often verbally confused Alice. And, in addition, his constant disappearances and reappearances are terribly distracting.

"How do you know I'm mad?" asks Alice.

"You must be or you wouldn't have come here," the cat says.

Alice then contradicts the cat when he claims to growl. "Call it what you like," he says. Then, in a clairvoyant moment, he casually mentions that he'll see Alice at the Queen's croquet game. At this point, Alice hasn't even been *invited* to the game, nor has she indicated any intention of going. But like the Frog-Footman, the Cheshire-Cat transfigures reality and anticipates events. He's not surprised that the baby became a pig; he's only uncertain whether Alice said "pig" or "fig." Ultimately, his smile is his most enduring and least confusing aspect. Alice complains that his vanishing and reappearing "so suddenly" make her dizzy. She asks him not to disappear; his response is to "slow down" his disappearance so that he appears to *dissolve*; in the end, only his grin remains, and then it too disappears. The Cheshire-Cat's smile is the embodiment of Wonderland's riddle; it is as famous and as enigmatic as Mona Lisa's smile.

Curiously, it is the Cheshire-Cat who offers Alice a "meaning" to Wonderland's chaos. Alice's curiosity has led her into a mad world, and she has begun to wonder if she herself is mad. She realizes that there is just a possibility that she may be mad! And the fact that Alice is, finally, *not* surprised at the cat's vanishing does indicate a kind of madness on her part. And after being told that the Mad Hatter and the March Hare are also mad, Alice *still* insists on meeting them. In her conversation with the cat, Alice tries to come to terms with madness, but it seems that she has no choice in the matter. All roads, as it were, lead to mad people, and she seems to be one of them. The cat's grin undermines her security in anything she hears because the connection between subject (cat) and attribute (grin) has been severed.

"Well," [Alice thought], "I've often seen a cat without a grin . . . but a grin without a cat! It's the most curious thing I ever saw in all my life."

Here is a smile without a face, without any substance—just a smile. The smile has become a nightmare of perplexity. Yet what the cat told Alice *is* logical; she *can* get somewhere by walking long enough in any direction. But it is not the answer to the question which Alice asked. Thus, the cat's responses to her inquiries are scaled to very different values than the values above-ground in Alice's familiar Victorian world. And looked at objectively, the Cheshire-Cat does not really accept Alice as an equal. He patronizes her gullibility as any adult might play with a child. In the end, Alice doesn't learn anything from him.

Soon, Alice finds the house of the March Hare. Since it is May, she reasons (a *wrong* thing to do in Wonderland), the Hare should be "mad" only in March. She nibbles at her mushroom until she becomes taller; increasing her size gives her more self-confidence, but she still has not learned that getting smaller or larger by such means will *not* enable her to deal with Wonderland any better.

CHAPTER VII

"A Mad Tea-Party"

Linguistic assaults are very much a part of the "polite bantering" in Wonderland. Often, traumatic and verbal violence seems just about to erupt all the time, breaking through the thin veneer of civilized behavior, but it rarely does. Alice reaches the March Hare's house in time for an outdoor tea-party. The tea-party turns out to be a *very* mad tea-party. In attendance are Alice, the March Hare, the Mad Hatter, and a Dormouse. All are indeed mad, except (perhaps) Alice and the sleepy Dormouse (who is only mad when he is awake). Alice has arrived just in time for tea, which is served at six o'clock. But it is *always* six o'clock, with no time to wash the dishes; thus, it is *always* tea time. In fact, the significant feature about this tea-party is that time has been frozen still. The idea of real, moving, passing time is non-existent.

The absense of time means that the Mad Tea-Party is trapped in a space without time. The world isn't turning, hands aren't moving around the clock, and the only "rotating" exists around the tea-party table. When the four have finished tea (although Alice gets none), they move to the next place-setting around the table. Dirty dishes accumulate, and there doesn't seem to be any substantive food. No one even seems to be taking tea. The Mad Hatter tells Alice that the Queen has accused him of murdering his friend Time; ever since the Mad Hatter and Time had a falling out, it has always been six o'clock. It's always tea time, and they have no time to wash the dishes between time for tea.

Alice typically does her best to cling to her *own* code of behavior (as always); she is *still* determined to "educate" the creatures to the rules of Victorian social etiquette. They protest her joining the party with cries of "No room! No room!" But Alice ignores them (she is larger now), and she sits down. The insanity of it all begins immediately when the March Hare offers her wine that doesn't exist. Alice complains, of course, about this lack of civility in offering her some non-existent wine. The March Hare counters that *she* was very rude to invite herself to their party. Her rules of etiquette completely fail her here. These creatures once again turn upside down all her principles of decorum.

"Your hair wants cutting," the Mad Hatter interrupts her at one point.

"You should learn not to make personal remarks," Alice says. "It's very rude."

Later, she violates her advice and impolitely interrupts the Mad Hatter. "Nobody asked *your* opinion," she says. "Who's making personal remarks now?" retorts the Mad Hatter.

Alice has been deflated and demoralized. The last above-ground rules of how to act and what to say seem to dissolve before her eyes. She *cannot* understand why they are acting this way!

Thus, the tea-party continues with endless cups of tea and a conversation of absolutely meaningless nonsense. Suddenly, the Mad Hatter asks Alice: "Why is a raven like a writing desk?"

At first glance, the riddle makes no sense as a logical question. And even the answer that Carroll provides elsewhere (the raven produces a few notes, all very flat, and it is never put the wrong end front) is nonsense. Presumably there should always be answers to any questions; at least, there were answers above-ground.

The Mad Tea-Party conversation repeats this miscommunication pattern like all the other absurd conversations that Alice has had with Wonderland creatures in previous chapters. She delightfully explains: "I'm glad they've begun asking riddles – I believe I can guess that."

"Do you mean that you think you can find out the answer to it?" asks the March Hare.

"Exactly so," says Alice.

"Then you should say what you mean," says the Hare.

Alice's confidence is shaken: "I do," she says, "at least – at least I mean what I say – that's the same thing you know."

But here, of course, Alice is speaking in the context of time's absence. There is no time. This is, even in Wonderland, "another world."

"Why," says the Hare, "you might just as well say that 'I see what I eat' is the same thing as 'I eat what I see!'" This is reverse logic – exactly right for Wonderland, but, of course, not correct above-ground.

Alice cannot make the creatures understand this, however, and finally she sighs. "I think you might do something better with time . . . than wasting it in asking riddles that have no answers." To this, the Hatter replies: "If you knew Time as well as I do . . . you wouldn't talk about wasting *it*. It's him."

Time is thus suddenly personified and becomes the source of much punning and comic relief. Alice participates in this nonsense in all seriousness, saying that she has to "beat time" when she learns music, even though she has "perhaps" never spoken to "him."

"Ah! That accounts for it," says the Mad Hatter. "He won't stand beating!"

Then the Mad Hatter launches into a satirical parody of another, famous children's verse: "Twinkle, twinkle little bat!" The bat is not the shining star of the Victorian poem, but a repulsive and morbid symbol of the ugly course of events about to begin. The Mad Hatter explains that his fight with Time and accusation of murder happened the last time that he was reciting that verse. So the disaster with Time is closely related to the Mad Hatter's distortion of the nursery rhyme. Filling his version with bats and flying tea-trays, the Mad Hatter's rhyme increases the comic personification of Time. The Mad Hatter has animated the inanimate star as a bat and has made an inanimate object *live*.

The Mad Tea-Party is filled with atrocious puns in conversation. The pun is determined by the coincidence of two words that sound so alike that relevant information is muddled. And here the play on words is a way of freeing meaning from conventional definition. The Dormouse, for instance, tells a story about three sisters who lived in a treacle well and were learning to "draw" treacle (molasses). Alice asks:

"But I don't understand. Where did they draw treacle from?"

"You can draw water out of a water-well," says the Mad Hatter, "so I should think you could draw treacle out of a treacle-well."

"But they were in the well," says Alice (very logically).

"Of course they were," says the Dormouse. "Well in."

The Dormouse's illogic continues to frustrate Alice. Playing on words that begin with the letter *M*, the Dormouse describes the sisters as *drawing* "all manner of things – everything that begins with an *M*, such as mousetraps, and the moon, and memory, and muchness – you know you say things are 'much of a muchness' – did you ever see such a thing as a drawing of a muchness!"

Alice stammers, and the Hatter cries, "Then you shouldn't talk."

With that rude remark, Alice storms away in disgust. She has *still* not succeeded in getting any closer to the reality she seeks. At the tea-party, she has not even received any tea *or* food. Her serving has been only a bitter course of verbal abuse and semantic teasing. Muchness indeed! The creatures are self-centered, argumentative and rude; they have violated all of the conventions of conversation that Alice has been taught to practice. All of these creatures in Wonderland have compounded the pain of Alice's psychological loss of place and time with their nonsense and cruel teasing.

As she leaves the table, Alice notices the other two attempting to drown the Dormouse in the teapot. His ritualistic death is, at least, a seemingly logical consequence of the Mad Hatter's ominous verse and Alice's departure. The Dormouse *should* have been hibernating instead of attending parties and telling anecdotes; dunking him seems to be sort of a realistic – if an absurd – way of forcing him back to "slumber." This will be, however, if they are successful, more than just a "slumber"; it will be death, "much of a muchness."

The Dormouse's fate serves as an appropriate conclusion to this chapter, for Alice enters another door and finds herself once again in the hallway with the glass table and the small doorway that leads to the beautiful garden. To try and reinforce the notion that Wonderland *must* have a hidden order, Alice first unlocks the door, and she then reduces her size by nibbling on a piece of the mushroom.

She has *finally* learned a lesson from her initial, frightening experience in Wonderland: she has been eating, drinking, and changing sizes, without thinking *first.*

CHAPTER VIII

"The Queen's Croquet-Ground"

At last, Alice finds herself in the garden that she has so long sought to explore. Far from being a wild Eden, though, the garden is well cultivated and tended. And now Alice meets a whole set of new creatures – this time, several animated playing cards. Immediately, she finds out that the Spades are, of course, the gardeners. And in spite of the Eden-like appearance, the garden has an aspect of "fear" in the air. Alice overhears three gardeners – the Two, the Five, and the Seven – talking about the Queen's threat to behead the Seven of Spades. They are painting the white roses red, an ominous color in view of their discussion.

Suddenly, the Queen and King of Hearts appear. They are followed by a suit of cards which represents the "royal retainers." The Clubs are the "police," the Diamonds are the "courtiers," and the Hearts make up the royal "peerage." The Queen sees Alice and the three Spade gardeners (who have thrown themselves flat on the ground so as to try and conceal their identity). The Queen asks Alice *who* the three cards are, and Alice replies tartly: "How should *I* know?"

This flippant answer throws the Queen into a rage; instantly she explodes with her infamous and beastly command: "Off with her head!"

"Nonsense," says Alice, very loudly.

The frequency and roaring of the Queen's threats reveal the terrible rule underlying the world of Wonderland. Execution, or the threat of execution, is indiscriminately announced – and canceled – in whimsical moments, with automatic reprieves. One may be sentenced to death without having committed a crime – indeed, without having received a verdict. In contradicting the Queen, Alice confronts the system of Wonderland *directly,* as a leading participant-actor; *she is no longer a detached observer.* Wonderland is now a world of cruelty, destruction, and annihilation, and Alice sees this, and already we can see the possibility of her emerging from it, smiling and unscathed.

52

The Queen orders the gardeners to be executed. Alice manages to save their lives, however, by hiding them in a flower pot. (Her fear seems to have been unfounded. The Gryphon tells her that nobody in Wonderland is ever executed.) There is more humor in the subsequent scenes. Note, too, that Wonderland is a "Queendom," instead of a Kingdom because the King is subordinate to the Queen. Now, familiar characters like the White Rabbit, the Duchess, and the Cheshire-Cat enter the croquet-garden. The croquet game again reverses the real-world division between life and inanimate objects as hedgehogs form the balls, the flamingoes the mallets, and the card-soldiers the hoops. The White Rabbit apprises Alice of her inherent danger in a whispered conversation. Even the Duchess, he says, is in jail under a sentence of execution for having boxed the Queen's ears. Alice learns all this but she seems *not* to be intimidated. In the next scene, the Cheshire-Cat demonstrates the violently repressive regime of Wonderland.

Because the cat is impertinent to the King, it is sentenced to be beheaded. But only the cat's head has materialized so the decapitation cannot be performed. The failed execution marks the slow disintegration of Wonderland in Alice's estimation. Within the character of the cat, Alice recognizes a fair and open mind. But he is fair and open—only to a limited degree. She tries to explain to the cat that the croquet game doesn't make sense because the game has "no rules." The cat, however, replies in such non-sequiturs as "How do you like the Queen?" Clearly, the cat can no more understand a game with no rules than he can understand a world where cats could *not* disappear and reappear in thin air. Alice mistakes the Cheshire-Cat for a friend and someone with whom she can relate on a real-world, logical level. Her assumption is wrong.

CHAPTERS IX—XII

"The Mock Turtle's Story," "The 'Lobster-Quadrille,'" "Who Stole the Tarts?" and "Alice's Evidence"

Alice's major problem with Wonderland continues to be her inability to completely penetrate what she thinks exists—that is, its "logic."

The Queen has a soldier fetch the Duchess at the close of the last chapter, and Alice finds the Duchess in a surprisingly good mood. Alice attributes, logically, her previous ill-temper to the Cook's pepper. "Maybe it's always pepper that makes people hot-tempered," she thinks, very much pleased at having believed that she has discovered a "new kind of rule," a rule of logic that exists in this strange world of Wonderland.

The Duchess, very much in the mold of a proper Victorian, finds a rule in *everything*, but they are rules and precepts which are nothing more than improvised absurdities: ". . . flamingoes and mustard both bite. And the moral of that is – 'Birds of a feather flock together.'" As this conversation takes place, the Duchess has seductively dug her hideous chin into Alice's shoulder, but their silly dialogue underlines the fun – and the entire world of nonsense – in Wonderland's satire on the nature of all "rules."

The mad Queen appears, and her presence – just her *presence* – is intimidating. The Duchess cowers and flies away from the garden. This form of bullying is a humorous evocation of the world of power relations. The Duchess flees from the Queen – and at that moment, all the croquet players and hoops have been placed under custody and sentenced to death! Only Alice, the King and the Queen are left to play the insane croquet game. Presumably, the Duchess could challenge the Queen's power at this point. But the Duchess is like Alice; each of them respects rank. So the "more humane" Duchess yields to the Queen of Hearts.

Next, Alice meets two of the most incredible creatures in Wonderland; the Gryphon (Griffin) and the Mock Turtle (whose name comes from veal soup). The two creatures listen sympathetically to Alice's story of her adventures in Wonderland. The Gryphon finds her story merely curious, but the Mock Turtle thinks that her verse is "uncommon nonsense." Alice quickly finds out the false nature of their initial sympathy. The Gryphon's intense, selfish sorrow is revealed finally as being just a fancy, and the Mock Turtle's sensitivity is a reflection of his fearful name – a reminder of his eventual fate as something's or someone's meal.

Carroll's satire in Wonderland is once again brought into play in the Mock Turtle's education. As a "real tortoise," he studied such things as: "Reeling and Writhing . . . and the different branches of Arithmetic – Ambition, Distraction, Uglification and Derision . . . and

Mystery . . . Seaography; then Drawling – the Drawling-master was an old conger-eel, that used to come once a week: he taught us drawling, stretching and fainting in Coils." A classical teacher taught the Mock Turtle "Laughing and Grief." And finally lessons were called lessons "because they lessen from day to day."

Chapters IX and X, thus, break with the pattern of Wonderland. At last, Alice finds one character who displays an absence of hostility. The Gryphon, for instance, is often tart but his intentions are at least outwardly sympathetic. The Mock Turtle and the Gryphon seem to confirm Alice's sense of Wonderland's peculiar disorder, and in Chapter X, "The 'Lobster-Quadrille,' " we have another sad account of a meal and a dance, told in mock heroic couplets.

Chapter XI ("Who Stole the Tarts?") and Chapter XII ("Alice's Evidence") reduce the above-ground facsimile of justice to a travesty. The one constant factor in the "enchanted garden" – the Queen's furious demand for executions – turns out to have *always* been ignored, as Alice learns from the Gryphon. In Chapter XI, the Knave of Hearts is brought to trial and accused of stealing tarts. Eating again becomes the method of someone's downfall.

The Knave of Hearts' trial becomes a pointless formality as soon as we hear the Queen's directive: "Sentence first – verdict afterward." The White Rabbit serves as Herald of the Court, thus fulfilling the symbolic role which he plays in introducing the story. The members of the Mad Tea-Party and the Duchess' cook are all brought in to give evidence. But the trial is completely lacking – in *rules, evidence,* and *justice.* The trial becomes yet another humorous illustration of Wonderland's assault on real-world semantics and linguistic principles.

"Take off your hat," the King tells the Hatter.

"It isn't mine," the Hatter says.

"If that's all you know about it, you may step down," the King tells him.

"I can't go no lower," says the Mad Hatter, "I'm on the floor, as it is."

All during this time, Alice is beginning to grow to her original size. When she reveals this to the Dormouse, he replies: "You've no right to grow here." Part of the fun at this point is that Alice seems to know all about court proceedings and the names of things, although she has never been in a court of justice. The purpose of the narrator in letting us know this fact is that it prepares us for her discomfort at the absurdity and insanity of the court proceedings.

In the final chapter, ironically entitled "Alice's Evidence," it is Alice who gets all the evidence she needs to rebel against the cruelty of Wonderland's trial. After observing the jurymen scribble nonsense as they take testimony, she decides that the nonsense has gone far enough. (In one funny scene, she takes juryman Bill the Lizard's pencil away from him, but he continues to write with his finger.)

Alice dramatically demonstrates her new subversive attitude. The Queen asserts without any evidence that the Knave has been proven guilty by the "evidence." "It doesn't prove anything of the sort," replies Alice. The only thing offered in evidence for the prosecution is the White Rabbit's vague poem, which (as Alice observes) *no one understands*. The Queen makes her usual command: "Sentence first—verdict afterward." Alice retorts: "Stuff and Nonsense!" The Queen sentences Alice, but by then Alice has grown to her full height. "Who cares for *you?*" Alice says. "You're nothing but a pack of cards!"

This loud proclamation signals her flight from Wonderland's anarchy to the sanity of above-ground. Alice emerges finally from her confused doubts about this mixed-up world of Wonderland. She rebels, and she leaves the world underneath the ground for the world of common sense and consciousness. Her "lesson," if it can be called that, is that she learns what she has already known. That is, she imposes her order on chaos, and, in consequence, her world of wonderful but unreal and strange and fanciful, glorious things is destroyed. After all, one cannot live long in a dream world. Such things as identity, sanity, laws, logic, and self-preservation have a price. To sustain them, Alice had to reject endless, timeless "possibilities." Her dream, in effect, ends just before a nightmare begins.

The narrator concludes the Wonderland dream: "So Alice got up and ran off, thinking while she ran, as well she might, what a wonderful dream it had been."

Alice wakes up on the lap of her sister filled with the images of Wonderland from her "curious dream." Thus, fantasy is transformed into memory; and any memory can seem real, and it will seem real, in its own way, to Alice, always.

CRITICAL ANALYSIS

Alice as a Character

Alice is reasonable, well-trained, and polite. From the start, she is a miniature, middle-class Victorian "lady." Considered in this way, she is the perfect foil, or counterpoint, or contrast, for all the *un*social, bad-mannered eccentrics whom she meets in Wonderland. Alice's constant resource and strength is her courage. Time and again, her dignity, her directness, her conscientiousness, and her art of conversation *all* fail her. But when the chips are down, Alice reveals something to the Queen of Hearts—that is: spunk! Indeed, Alice has all the Victorian virtues, including a quaint capacity for rationalization; yet it is Alice's *common sense* that makes the quarrelsome Wonderland creatures seem perverse in spite of what they consider to be their "adult" identities.

Certainly, Alice fits no conventional stereotype; she is neither angel nor brat. She simply has an overwhelming curiosity, but it is matched by restraint and moderation. She is balanced in other ways, too. To control her growth and shrinking, she only "samples" the cake labeled "EAT ME." And never is there a hint that she would seek to use her size advantage to control her fate and set dictatorial rules of behavior for Wonderland. The Caterpillar takes offense when she complains of being three inches tall. And the Duchess is unreasonable, coarse, and brutal. But in each case, their veneer of "civility" is either irrational or transparent. The Caterpillar finds mirth in teasing Alice with his pointed, formal, verb games, and the rude Duchess mellows into a corrupt "set of silly rules." Yet, behind their playfulness, Alice senses resentment and rage. It is not so much that Alice is kept "simple" so as to throw into relief the monstrous aspects of Wonderland characters. Rather, it is that Alice, as she conceives of her personality in a dream, *sees herself* as simple, sweet, innocent, and confused.

Some critics feel that Alice's personality and her waking life are reflected in Wonderland; that may be the case. But the story itself is independent of Alice's "real world." Her personality, as it were, stands alone in the story, and it must be considered in terms of the Alice character in Wonderland.

A strong moral consciousness operates in all of Alice's responses to Wonderland, yet on the other hand, she exhibits a child's insensitivity in discussing her cat Dinah with the frightened Mouse in the pool of tears. Generally speaking, Alice's simplicity owes a great deal to Victorian feminine passivity and a repressive domestication. Slowly, in stages, Alice's reasonableness, her sense of responsibility, and her other good qualities will emerge in her journey through Wonderland

and, especially, in the trial scene. Her list of virtues is long: curiosity, courage, kindness, intelligence, courtesy, humor, dignity, and a sense of justice. She is even "maternal" with the pig/baby. But her constant and universal human characteristic is simple *wonder* – something with which all children (and the child that still lives in most adults) can easily identify with.

THEMES

Alice in Wonderland provides an inexhaustible mine of literary, philosophical, and scientific themes. Here are some general themes which the reader may find interesting and of some use in studying the work.

Abandonment/Loneliness

Alice's initial reaction after falling down the rabbit-hole is one of extreme loneliness. Her curiosity has led her into a kind of Never-Never Land, over the edge of Reality and into a lonely, very alien world. She is further lost when she cannot establish her identity. Physically, she is lost; psychologically, she also feels lost. She cannot get her recitations right, and she becomes even more confused when her arithmetic (a subject she believed to be unchanging and solid) fails her. Every attempt to establish a familiar basis of identity creates only the sense of being lost – absolutely lost. Alice becomes, to the reader, a mistreated, misunderstood, wandering waif. Trapped in solitude, she finds herself lapsing into soliloquies that reflect a divided, confused, and desperate self.

The Child-Swain

Alice is the most responsible "character" in the story; in fact, she is the only real person and the only "true" character. At most, the other creatures are antagonists, either a bit genial or cruel, depending on how they treat Alice at any given point in the story. Alice's innocence makes her a perfect vehicle of social criticism a la Candide. In her encounters, we see the charmingly pathetic ingénue – a child whose only purpose is to escape the afflictions around her. By implication, there is the view that a child's perception of the world is the only sane one. Conversely, to grow and mature leads to inevitable corruption, to sexuality, emotionalism, and adult hypocrisy. The child as an inno- cent, sympathetic object has obvious satirical utility, but only to the point that the child must extend sympathy herself – and Alice fails to do this when she describes her cat Dinah to the Mouse, and later when she confesses to having eaten eggs to the frightened mother pigeon.

Children and Animals

In an age such as our own, where philosophers earnestly debate the rights of animals, or whether machines can "think," we cannot escape the child's affinity for animals. And in Wonderland, except for the Gryphon, none of the animals are of a hostile nature that might lead Alice to any harm. (And the Gryphon is a mythical animal so he doesn't count as a "true" animal.) Most of the Wonderland animals are the kind one finds in middle-class homes, pet shops, and in children's cartoons. Although they may not seem so in behavior, most of them are, really, pets. Alice feels a natural identity with them, but her relationship ultimately turns on her viewing them as *adults.* So her identity with the animals has a lot to do with her size in relation- ship to adults. Alice emphasizes this point when she observes that some ugly children might be improved if they were pigs. In her obser- vation lies the acceptance of a common condition of children and animals: each is personified to a degree. Thus, it is not surprising that in the world of the child, not only animals, but dolls, toys, plants, insects, and even playing cards have the potential to be personified by children (or adults).

Death

Growing up in Wonderland means the death of the child, and although Alice certainly remains a child through her physical changes in size – in other ways, death never seems to be far away in Wonderland. For example, death is symbolized by the White Rab- bit's fan which causes Alice to *almost* vanish; death is implied in the discussion of the Caterpillar's metamorphosis. And death permeates the morbid atmosphere of the "enchanted garden." The Queen of Hearts seems to be the Goddess of Death, always yelling her single, barbarous, indiscriminate, "Off with their heads!"

Nonsense

One of the key characteristics of Carroll's story is his use of language. Much of the "nonsense" in *Alice* has to do with transpositions, either of mathematical scale (as in the scene where Alice multiplies incorrectly) or in the scrambled verse parodies (for example, the Father William poem). Much of the nonsense effect is also achieved by directing conversation to parts of speech rather than to the meaning of the speakers—to definitions rather than to indications. When Alice asks the Cheshire-Cat which way to go, he replies that she should, first, know where she's going. The Frog-Footman tells her not to knock on the door outside the Duchess' house; he can only open the door when he is inside (though Alice, of course, manages to open the door from the outside). And some of the nonsense in Wonderland is merely satirical, such as the Mock Turtle's education. But the nature of nonsense is much like chance, and rules to decipher it into logical meaning or sense patterns work against the principal intent of Carroll's purpose—that is, he wanted his nonsense to be random, senseless, unpredictable, and without rules.

Nature and Nurture

The structure of a dream does not lend itself to resolution. A dream simply is a very different kind of "experience." In this sense, Alice does not really evolve into a higher understanding of her adventure. She has the *memory* of Wonderland but she brings nothing "real" from Wonderland—only her memory of it. This is a powerful testament to the influence of her domestication. In Alice's case, good social breeding is more important than her natural disposition. But if Alice leaves Wonderland without acquiring any lasting, truly worthwhile knowledge, neither can she give any wisdom to the creatures whom she has met there. Nature, in each case, sets limits on the ability to assimilate experiences.

In the Caucus-race, for instance, the race depicts the absurdity of democracy. Yet, Alice's critical attitude—a product of her class education—is also satirized. The object of the race is to have everyone dry off; so it doesn't matter *who* wins or loses, and clearly the outcome of the race is irrelevant. To think otherwise, as Alice does, is absurd. The point of the running about is to dry off, which, incidentally, makes it equally absurd to call moving about for that purpose a "race."

Wonderland offers a peculiar view of Nature. For one thing, all the animals have obviously been educated. There is literally not a "stupid" one in the bunch (unless it is the puppy or the pig/baby). In general, the basic condition common to all the creatures is not ignorance – but madness, for which there seems to be no appropriate remedy. A Victorian reader must have wondered how the animals were "trained"; after all, the assumptions that Alice makes all rest on her "training." On this point, however, the reader can only speculate.

In Wonderland, much of the fun depends on the confusion of "training." Nature and natural feelings seem to more often than not mean danger or potential violence. (But except for the puppy and the pig/baby, there are no natural creatures, however much natural feelings are expressed.) The Duchess, for example, seems to be only the epitome of rage; she conveys a kind of sadistic delight in digging her chin into Alice's shoulder; anger even seems to motivate her didactic morals (that is, "Flamingoes and mustard both bite.").

Finally, nature seems superior to nurture in Wonderland, as the personification of beasts seems to be no improvement on the actual beasts themselves. The pig, for example, is a more content creature *as a pig,* for the baby was not happier when it was a *baby.*

Justice

Although there are plenty of "rules," the laws of Wonderland seem a parody of real justice. The Queen of Hearts, for example, thinks nothing of violating the law which protects people from illegal prosecution; she seeks the head of the Knave of Hearts for having been only *accused* of stealing the tarts. Thus, the Queen violates the spirit of the law against stealing to satisfy the logical necessity that *every* trial must have an execution. The spirit of the law is, so to speak, sacrificed to satisfy the reversibility of the symbolic letter of her logic. In the croquet game, anyone can be executed for reasons known *only* to the sovereign Queen, who acts as though she is a divinity with the power to take or give life. Under a monarchy, the monarchs are above the law. In Wonderland, however, the monarch's will is flaunted when the command is to execute someone. Ignoring the Queen's command to behead someone is a matter of survival as well as justice.

The trial of the Knave of Hearts satirizes both too much law and law by personal edict. Someone may have stolen the tarts, and it may well have been the Knave. But the offense is trivial, and the sentence is only a joke. One of the problems with the law in any context is its application. When the law ceases to promote harmony, then its purpose as a regulator of human affairs is subverted. In Wonderland, the idea of a law seems ridiculous because the *operative principle* of Wonderland is *chaos*. Injustice, then, is a logical consequence of living in Wonderland. The rule of the strongest person must be the law — that is, the law of anarchy. The trial of the Knave is proof of this woeful state of affairs. Fortunately, Alice is the strongest of the lot, and she overthrows the cruel Queen's sentence of execution and the savage kangaroo court. There is no way to change the law because no "law" exists. By her rebellion, Alice serves both the cause of sanity and justice.

Time and Space

Time, in the sense of duration, exists in Wonderland only in a psychological and artistic sense. When we ordinarily conceive of time, we think of units of duration — that is, hours, minutes, and seconds; or days, weeks, months, and years. We may also think of getting older and having lived from a certain date. We assume that the time reflected on a clock and our age are essentially the same kind of process. But a clock may repeat its measure of duration, whereas *we* have only *one* lifetime. Our age is therefore a function of an irreversible, psychological sense of duration. We live in the conscious knowledge that we can never return to a given point in the past, as we might adjust a clock for daylight savings time. Our personal, psychological time is absolute and irreversible. And that is the kind of time that creatures like the Mad Hatter employ in Wonderland. (We never know whether the White Rabbit uses a mechanistic time, only that he has a watch.)

When Alice looks at the Mad Hatter's watch, she sees a date, but she sees neither hours nor minutes. Because Time and the Mad Hatter do not get along, Time has "frozen" the tea-party at six o'clock. But it turns out that time is also reversed so that a year has the duration of an hour and vice versa. Reckoned in hour-lengths, the tea-party must go on for at least a year (unless Time and the Mad Hatter make up their quarrel). But because of psychological time, the creatures are able to leave and return to the tea-party. And because of psychological time, Wonderland's experience comes to an end, and just as our uniquely, individual lives will one day end, so will our nightmares and dreams.

ESSAY QUESTIONS

Long Essays

1. Relate aspects of enchantment to the nostalgia that Alice experiences in Wonderland. Why is Alice both fascinated and frustrated by her encounters below-ground?

2. Describe some of the ways that Carroll achieves humor at Alice's expense.

3. Give an analysis of the use of nonsense in *Alice*.

4. How does the question "Who am I?" relate to the wish to eat and the fear of being eaten in *Alice*?

Short Essays

1. Describe the White Rabbit's function in *Alice*.

2. What is the significance of the Cheshire-Cat in the Queen's Croquet-Ground scene?

3. Compare the Duchess' lullaby to the "You Are Old, Father William" verse.

4. Explain the sentiment of the Mouse's long tale, the Mock Turtle's story and the "Lobster-Quadrille."

SELECTED BIBLIOGRAPHY

AUDEN, W. H. "The Man Who Wrote Alice," *New York Times Book Review*, 28 February 1954, p. 4.

BERNADETTE, DORIS. "Alice Among the Professors," *Western Humanities Review,* V (1950), 239-47.

BURPEE, LAWRENCE J. "Alice Joins the Immortals," *Dalhousie Review,* XXI (1941), 194-204.

CHESTERTON, G. K. "Lewis Carroll," in *A Handful of Authors,* New York, 1953, pp. 112-19.

DARTON, F. J. HARVEY. *Children's Books in England: Five Centuries of Social Life,* second edition, Cambridge, 1958.

FLESHER, JACQUELINE. "The Language of Nonsense in *Alice,*" *Yale French Studies,* XLIII (1970), 128-44.

GREEN, ROGER LANCELYN. "The Real Lewis Carroll," *Quarterly Review,* CCXCII (1954), 85-97.

HUBBELL, GEORGE SHELTON. "The Sanity of Wonderland," *Sewanee Review,* XXXV (1927), 387-98.

HUDSON, DEREK. *Lewis Carroll,* London, 1954.

KENT, MURIEL. "The Art of Nonsense," *Cornhill,* CXLIX (1934), 478-87.

LENNON, FLORENCE BECKER. *Victoria Through the Looking Glass: The Life of Lewis Carroll,* revised edition, New York, 1962.

LEVIN, HARRY. "Wonderland Revisited," *Kenyon Review,* XXVII (1965), 591-616.

MACNEICE, LOUIS. "The Victorians," in *Varieties of Parable,* Cambridge, 1965.

MUIR, PERCY. *English Children's Books 1600-1900,* London, 1954.

PARTRIDGE, ERIC. "The Nonsense Words of Edward Lear and Lewis Carroll," in *Here, There and Everywhere,* London, 1950, pp. 162-88.

RACKIN, DONALD. "Corrective Laughter: Carroll's *Alice* and Popular Children's Literature of the Nineteenth Century," *Journal of Popular Culture,* I (1967), 243-55.

SEWELL, ELIZABETH. *The Field of Nonsense,* London, 1952.

THODY, PHILIP. "Lewis Carroll and the Surrealists," *Twentieth Century,* CLXIII (1958), 427-34.

WAUGH, EVELYN. "Carroll and Dodgson," *Spectator,* CLXIII (1939), 511.

WEAVER, WARREN. "Alice's Adventures in Wonderland: Its Origins and Its Author," *Princeton Library Chronicle,* XIII (1951), 1-17.

WHITE, ALISON. "Alice After a Hundred Years," *Michigan Quarterly Review,* IV (1965), 261-64.

WILSON, EDMUND. "C. L. Dodgson: The Poet-Logician," in *The Shores of Light,* New York, 1952, pp. 540-50.

WOOD, JAMES P. *The Snark Was a Boojum: A Life of Lewis Carroll,* New York, 1966.

WOOLF, VIRGINIA. "Lewis Carroll," in *The Moment, and Other Essays,* New York, 1949, pp. 81-83.